Trojan Horse
How the New Age Movement Infiltrates the Church

Samantha Smith and
Brenda Scott

HUNTINGTON HOUSE PUBLISHERS

Huntington House Publishers
P.O. Box 53788
Lafayette, Louisiana 70505
1-800-749-4009

Library of Congress Card Catalogue Number
93-77443
ISBN 1-56384-040-5

Dedication

—to our families for their patience and prayers;

—to our friends for their encouragement;

—to fellow researchers for critical information; and

—to Cliff Dudley, who gave us the vision.

Special
Acknowledgment

We wish to express appreciation to Claris Van Kuiken for sharing her valuable research and assisting in the composition of the manuscript, and for her efforts to battle New Age heresy within the Body of Christ.

Contents

Preface

The two of us came together, through a strange series of circumstances, out of a deep concern for the Body of Christ. Our backgrounds, though varied, provide some common attributes. We are researchers, writers, lecturers, and sisters in Christ, whose joint purpose is to expose the seductive heresies that have been brought into the church by Madeleine L'Engle and her associates.

Had L'Engle remained in the secular realm, this book would not have been written. Further, we do not wish to attack anyone's character, but we cannot sit by and watch this apostasy grow like a cancer within the Body. It is our prayerful desire that Truth will be revealed and will set many free.

Despite her blatant denial of the basic tenets of the faith, Madeleine L'Engle's influence has deeply penetrated mainstream Christianity. Under the guise of "Christian literature," this prolific writer has been instrumental in introducing New Age/occult concepts and techniques into the church. The deception, unfortunately, has been so successful that otherwise discerning congregations and pastors have fallen into the snare that she and others have laid.

Deeply concerned, we've approached some of the leaders in the Christian community regarding her heresies, only to have our concerns dismissed as insignificant. One researcher was even asked to leave her own congregation. There is currently an on-going battle raging within the Christian Reformed Church (CRC) over the teachings that have been introduced into congregations, schools, and universities by Madeleine L'Engle.

How could it be that the Church, the Body of Christ, would be put into the position of having to debate the merits of practices and teachings condemned by God Himself? Through what door has this heresy entered the church, and how widespread is it?

> When you enter the land the Lord your God is giving you, do not learn to imitate the detestable ways of the nations there. Let no one be found among you who sacrifices his son or daughter in the fire, who practices divination or sorcery, interprets omens, engages in witchcraft, or casts spells or who is a medium or spiritist or who consults the dead. Anyone who does these things is detestable to the Lord . . .
>
> —Deut. 18:9-12a

Introduction

"If I wanted to write a statement of what I believe, I'd go off and get ordained. I'm a storyteller. I think my talent is for story. As a storyteller, my first job is to tell a story. **The theology is underneath** if you want to find it. You can say more in story than you can in a sermon."
—Madeleine L'Engle from *The Wittenberg Door*, December Issue, 1986, p. 25

"All my life through stories, those I read, and those I write, I have been building (intuitively, rather than consciously) a **theology** . . . the word about God . . ."
—Madeleine L'Engle, *Trailing Clouds of Glory*, p. 13

Popular "Christian" author of both fiction and nonfiction for all ages, Madeleine L'Engle most definitely has a strong theology of her own, which she skillfully weaves throughout all her books. From her feminist perch, she takes aim at the male gender of God, calling Him "the paternalistic male chauvinist pig Old Testament God. . . ."[1] She then proceeds to rewrite Scripture, discarding those teachings that conflict with her personal beliefs, and develops a completely different gospel.

Because of her radical departure from traditional Christian theology, L'Engle's writings have sparked a wave of controversy across the nation. Some claim her works present a "strong, underlying Christian message." Others believe she is promoting New Age thought and occult practices.

L'Engle is best known for her Newbery Award winning book, *A Wrinkle in Time*. It has been translated into fifteen different languages and is on recommended reading lists for public schools, private schools, and American Christian Schools International. This book has introduced millions of readers worldwide to her *theology*.

A talented writer and speaker, Madeleine L'Engle has been published and promoted by numerous magazines, including *Today's Christian Woman*, *Christianity Today*, *Christian Home and School*, the *Youth Ministry Catalogue*, *Church Teachers*, and the Christian Reformed Church's publication, the *Banner*.

She also appears frequently as a guest on "The Chicago Sunday Evening Club" television program and was a featured speaker at Bill and Gloria Gaither's "Praise Gathering" in Indianapolis, Indiana, during November of 1991. She has been featured as the keynote speaker at a United Methodist Women's Conference in Boston and appeared at Immanuel Congregational Church (United Church of Christ) in Hartford, Connecticut, and at Cherry Hills Community Church in Denver, Colorado.

Madeleine L'Engle has also lectured on Christian college campuses such as: Bethel Baptist Institute in Minnesota, Calvin College (Grand Rapids, Michigan), Presbyterian Wilson College (Pennsylvania), and Wheaton College (Wheaton, Illinois), where she received an honorary doctorate degree. Her writings are housed in a special collection in Wheaton's library, placing a mark of rare significance upon them. She was given a standing ovation at the Japanese Christian Education Center in Japan and was requested to speak at Stoneybrook Christian School (Long Island, New York).

Her book, *A Wrinkle in Time*, was influential in the formation of a school of "new thought," based on her concept of "tessering," the occult practice of astral projection. The Tessract School, a model alternative-school system located in Paradise Valley, Arizona, is poised to reproduce itself all around the country.

L'Engle repeatedly claims, "I know nothing about the New Age movement, nor do I care to."[2] Yet she is author-in-residence and assistant librarian at the Cathedral of St. John the Divine in New York City, where she also serves as a lay preacher. The Cathedral was credited in the *New Age Journal* as being the "Miracle on 112th Street." It houses Shinto and Native American shrines, has displayed a female figure of Christ called "Christa," and performs T'ai Chi rituals and Earth Masses. David Spangler, one of the world's most admired New Age teachers, goes there frequently to perform Eucharist. David Spangler believes that Christ is the same force as Lucifer.

Omega, a New Age Institute for holistic studies, lists Madeleine L'Engle as a faculty member, along with her close friend, "New Age" psychologist, M. Scott Peck.[3] This organization features such courses as: shamanism, out-of-body experiences or astral projection, Tarot methods of fortune telling, earth worship, psychic abilities, Yoga, Tantric Yoga (a sexual form of black magic), homosexuality, and astrology.

Other leading New Age figures she endorses, quotes, and promotes include: Marilyn Ferguson, author of "the watershed New Age classic," *The Aquarian Conspiracy*; physicist Fritjof Capra, author of the Bantam New Age book *The Tao of Physics*; and Lawrence LeShan, author of *The Medium, the Mystic and the Physicist* and New Age-labeled book, *How to Meditate.*

When confronted with legitimate concerns about her beliefs, L'Engle charges that those who criticize her books have "obviously never read them." Instead, continues her rebuttal, they are fundamentalists looking for "key words" and attacking her out of fear. She compares her opponents to Hitler, who "began by burning books and ended by burning people"—a typical strategy for anyone who does not wish to submit their writings to the scrutiny of others.

We have read and carefully examined her works and attended some of her lectures. We have also studied her personal interviews in many different publications and have extensively researched her writings, comparing them to the Holy Bible and to New Age/occult teachings.

God warns, "Woe to them who call evil good, and good evil; that put darkness for light and light for darkness. . . ." (Isa. 5:20). Occult writings have always twisted everything upside down. Evil is good, and good is evil. Light is dark, and dark is light. It is important for Christians to remember that Satan counterfeits himself as an "angel of light" and that "his servants masquerade as servants of righteousness" (II Cor. 11:14, 15).

Because of the nature of Madeleine L'Engle's writings, we have chosen to place her books in the category of the occult. Not only do *we* categorize her works as "occult material," but some libraries and esoteric writers stamp that label on them as well.

For example, her book, *A Wrinkle In Time*, is listed in the *New Age Guide* as well as in Linda Goodman's book, *Star Signs, the Secret Codes of the Universe: A Practical Guide for the New Age*, under the heading "For reading involving the general occult field."

We found that even the Allen County Library in Fort Wayne, Indiana, has placed *Wrinkle* under the category of the "Supernatural" and sandwiched it in between *The Satanic Bible* and *Rosemary's Baby*.

This book is not intended to discredit Madeleine L'Engle's character. However, because of the deadly nature of her doctrines and the fact that her theology has so deeply penetrated the Christian community, we felt compelled to expose them for what they truly are. The Scriptures warn us ". . . do not believe every spirit; but test the spirits to see whether they are from God, because many false prophets have gone out into the world" (I John 4:1).

The Apostle Paul commended the Bereans for examining the Scriptures daily to see if what he proclaimed was true (Acts 17:11). We encourage the readers to do likewise and to "contend for the faith that was once entrusted to the saints" (Jude 1:3).

Samantha Smith
Brenda Scott

CHAPTER ONE

0000000000000000000000000000000000000000000000

Fantasy? Or Occult 101

Madeleine L'Engle is probably best known through-out the world for her *Time Trilogy*, which consists of *A Wrinkle in Time*, *A Wind in the Door*, and *A Swiftly Tilting Planet*. These "fantasy" novels are centered around two youngsters, Charles Wallace and his older sister, Meg. Growing from childhood into adolescence and adult-hood, Charles and Meg are caught in many struggles between good and evil. Readers are told that "good" al-ways prevails. But what is the "good" that helps them win the battles? It is the use of psychic powers, which L'Engle strangely describes as "love."

Those "psychic powers" that run throughout her tril-ogy include ESP, mental telepathy, clairvoyance, astral travel (out-of-body experience), scrying (a form of divina-tion and fortune-telling), runes, and communication with the dead. Although God condemns such practices, L'Engle portrays them as "God's gifts," switching evil for good and undermining the Word of God.

Critiquing the *Time Trilogy* in the *Children's Litera-ture Review*, writer Gary D. Schmidt concurs: "Between the second and third novels nine years pass, so that in *A Swiftly Tilting Planet*, Meg is married and pregnant and Charles Wallace has made it into adolescence with as-tonishing intuitive powers . . . their *psychic powers* and familial relationships are solidly based on what has gone before" (emphasis added).

Central to the theme of the three novels are Madeleine L'Engle's concepts of the occult practices of "kything" and "tessering." "Kything," as defined by L'Engle, is "ESP"[1] or "mental telepathy,"[2] depending on which book you read.

ESP (extra sensory perception) is described in *The Concise Lexicon of the Occult* as "the transfer of thoughts from one mind into another; mind-to-mind communication; thought reading." Similarly, clairvoyance, a form of ESP, is "in spiritualism, the extraordinary power to perceive objects or events that are out of the range of the average human senses."[3]

L'Engle says that kything "goes much further" than ESP.[4] She's right; it does. Kything involves communication with the dead, plants, rocks, trees, and animals.

A book called *Kything: The Art of Spiritual Presence* (Paulist Press, 1988), by Louis N. Savary and Patricia H. Berne, was dedicated to L'Engle for giving a name to a large number of occult practices, describing them as "kything." In this book, we discovered an occult smorgasbord, including directions for communicating with the deceased, the dead saints, your dead beloved, Christ, animals, flowers, and you-name-it.

Kything also carries L'Engle's endorsement on the front cover. She says, "The whole book is full of wonderful encouragement for people who are willing to open themselves in love. . . . It's a beautiful book."

Occult writings often twist everything. In our ongoing study of mysticism/occultism/spiritualism, we often find that the authors deny what they are actually teaching. Strangely enough, many readers fall prey to this deception when the teachings are disguised as something spiritual or "Christian."

Although the authors of *Kything*, Savary and Berne, deny any affiliation with the occult, a quick study of what is promoted in their book lands anyone smack in the middle of techniques and philosophies found throughout occult literature. New Age thought (which is promoted throughout the book) is nothing more than the revival of ancient occultism.

Spiritual Revolution

Kything authors Savary and Berne *admit* to being part of a "spiritual revolution" that is exploding throughout the world. In the preface, they write, "Teilhard de Chardin's conspiracy is about getting millions of people to be lovingly joined at the level of spirit for the transformation of the world."

In 1980, Marilyn Ferguson became a kind of spokesperson for this revolutionary conspiracy called for by Teilhard de Chardin. Reporting in her book *The Aquarian Conspiracy*, which is the blueprint of the contemporary New Age movement, she described "a leaderless but powerful network were spontaneously uniting as conspirators for the sake of the earth . . ." Savary and Berne go on to boast, "both of us recognize ourselves as members of this conspiracy."And, L'Engle has endorsed the *whole book*?

Ferguson's *Aquarian Conspiracy* points out that some are open in their advocacy of the New Age movement, but that others "are quiet about their involvement, believing they can be more effective if they are not identified with ideas that have all too often been misunderstood."[5]

Is this why L'Engle says she knows nothing about the New Age movement, yet promotes it? We were more than a little surprised when we saw that Ishtar Films credited Wheaton College along with the Cathedral of St. John the Divine (considered by some to be the most occult spot in America) for their involvement with the film "Star-Gazer."[6]

Kything and Tessering

Have you ever wished you could project your spirit to another place without being seen? Would you like to make contact with someone without their knowing it? Plant an idea in his or her mind or change their feelings toward you? If you wish to

spiritually visit a lost love, an old friend, or, per-
haps, someone who has done you harm, Astral
Travel is the answer to your prayers. (Lady
Terezina, California Astrology Association)

Charles Wallace, one of L'Engle's favorite characters,
must be a kindred spirit to Lady Terezina. In *Swiftly
Tilting Planet*, Gaudior the unicorn helps him to "go
Within," to enter others' minds and bodies. Throughout
the plot, he and Meg employ astral travel, telepathy, and
a Welsh rune to save the universe from annihilation by
a mad dictator. Wallace defuses the enemy by going back
in time (with the help of the friendly time-and-space
hopping unicorn) and altering his ancestry and the course
of history. (Does this sound familiar?)

Charles and Meg enter what L'Engle refers to as the
"fifth dimension." This is a "tesseract." ". . . You can
travel through space without having to go the long way
around."[7] The *Donning International Encyclopedic Psychic Dictionary* defines the fifth dimension as the "Kingdom of the Mind, a type of cosmic consciousness one can
enter through altered states."

L'Engle suggests that tessering, or astral travel, could
become the preferred mode of travel in the future. In
Walking on Water: Reflections on Faith and Art, L'Engle
writes, "For short distances, the people fly; for longer
distances, they sit and meditate and then (as Meg Murray
would say) they tesser and they are there."[8]

L'Engle seems concerned that we human beings are
restricted, in our human forms, to time and space. She
teaches that we can overcome this handicap by engaging
in mystical contemplation. L'Engle herself uses twenti-
eth century mystics to help her in meditation and contemplation.[9] Subsequently, she makes this interesting
proposition: "We are not meant to be any more restricted
than Jesus was during his sojourn with us here on this
earth. If we take seriously that during the time of his
Incarnation he was truly man, truly human as we are,
then anything he did in his lifetime is available to us,
too."[10]

She goes on, "Am I suggesting that we really ought to be able to walk upon water? That there are (and not just in fantasies) easier and faster ways to travel than by jet and car? Yes, I am. There are too many stories of mystics being able to move hundreds of miles through the power of contemplation for us to be able to toss them aside."[11] L'Engle does not reveal that these mystics who experience such phenomena are involved in occult practices.

Madeleine L'Engle's occult/esoteric beliefs are hidden within volumes of fiction and non-fiction. That's exactly what she says "occult" means—"hidden."

Psychic Powers

Madeleine L'Engle would have Christians believe that occult psychic powers, if used for good, are not from Satan but from God himself. She writes in *And It Was Good*, "Human beings can use magic, sometimes for good, sometimes for evil; it has great power. . . . Magic is simply using what God has created, using it to do the things God created it to do. . . . Magic becomes bad when a human being takes the credit for it. The focus should be on God, the Giver of the gift."[12] But God did not give the gift of magic to the world, he condemned it.

In *Trailing Clouds of Glory, Spiritual Values in Children's Literature*, L'Engle mocks the church's "extreme right branch" for its condemnation of the "evils of witchcraft." She states:

> There is a lot of emphasis today, particularly among the more extreme right branches of the church, on the evils of witchcraft. Any book that mentions witches, or magic, or ghosts is automatically to be taken from the shelves. . . . Must we remove the Bible from the shelves because it contains not only ghosts and witches but incest and murder and lust and rape? We human beings tend to distort and misuse the original goodness of creation, but that does not make the original good less good, nor the marvelousness less marvelous.[13]

Why is she so worried about people banning books on witchcraft and magic? She certainly wouldn't have been pleased with the new Christian converts in Ephesus who had previously practiced sorcery. After their conversion, they burned their occult scrolls publicly! (Acts 19:17-20).

Going back to *Trailing Clouds of Glory*, L'Engle then gives a short excerpt from Ursula Le Guin's* book, *A Wizard of Earthsea*, which promotes sorcery. In the story, the wizard, called the Master Chanter, teaches Ged the "Lays of Wisdom" and spell after spell. But the wizard warns, "'A wizard's power of changing and of summoning can shake the world. It is dangerous, that power. It is most perilous. It must follow knowledge, and serve need.'"[14]

This warning is sounded by many occultists. For example, Linda Goodman writes in her New Age/occult book, *Star Signs*, "Mystical knowledge is power, and power will always tend to corrupt. Spiritual wisdom is the priceless key of those who earnestly desire to help others, as well as to attain personal joy and happiness—and is equally the dangerous master of those who wish to control others, who seek only personal benefit. . . . Esoteric mysteries must be approached cautiously, with reverence and compassion. . . ."[15]

---

*Ursula K. Le Guin enthusiastically endorses the book *Drawing Down the Moon*, by Margot Adler. Adler, a well-known reporter for PBS, "has been a priestess of Wicca for 18 years and is an Elder in the Covenant of the Goddess," according to Jean Houston's Oasis Center, a New Age association and mystery school located in Chicago. Houston herself promotes L'Engle's concept of kything in her workshops all around the country.

Adler's book is a classic work on paganism: a handbook on "witches, druids, Goddess-worshippers, and other pagans in history today." Along with L'Engle's *A Wrinkle in Time*, LeGuin's book, *A Wizard of Earthsea*, is listed in the *New Age Guide*, a resource book for those interested in becoming a part of the New Age.

Ursula Le Guin is also on the board of directors for *Parabola*, a New Age magazine.

Powers gained through the use of occult techniques, whether used for "good" or evil, come from the same source. This is probably the only statement that both the Bible and books on magic could agree on. As Anton LaVey, head of the Worldwide Church of Satan, states, "White magic is supposedly utilized for good or unselfish purposes, and black magic, we are told, is used only for selfish or evil reasons. Satanism draws no such dividing line. Magic is magic."[16]

God makes no distinctions, either. Deuteronomy 18:9-13 says:

> When you enter the land the Lord your God is giving you, do not learn to imitate the detestable ways of the nations there. Let no one be found among you who sacrifices his son or daughter in the fire, who practices divination or sorcery, interprets omens, engages in witchcraft, or casts spells or who is a medium or spiritist or who consults the dead. Anyone who does these things is detestable to the Lord, and because of those detestable practices the Lord your God will drive out those nations before you. You must be blameless before the Lord your God.

Madeleine L'Engle denies that these are the words of a loving Creator. She does not believe in a God who would drive out the nations because of their own religious beliefs. In *Sold into Egypt*, she writes,

> All through Scripture, the revelation of God and the people's understanding of God change. In the early chapters there are two quite different ways of looking at God, as there are two Creation stories, and two stories of the forming of Adam and Eve. There was a tribal god, who was one god among many gods. This tribal god was the warrior god of the patriarchs, who would expel the heathen from their own land so that his own people could occupy it, because the heathen were "them" and the tribal god wanted "us" to have the land.[17]

Why would L'Engle teach that the God who would drive out the nations who practiced witchcraft and sorcery is a "tribal" god? Why does she continually try to discredit the God of Abraham, Isaac, and Jacob as a creation of a chauvinistic society? Is Madeleine L'Engle uncomfortable because she condones the very same occult practices that God hates?

L'Engle's view of a "tribal" god and of dual creation accounts sounds incredibly like the teachings of New Age guru Joseph Campbell, as recorded in his book, *The Power of Myth.* "In the Bible, in the beginning, God was simply the most powerful god among many. He is just a local tribal god. . . . There are two creation stories in the Bible."[18] Surprising? Not really. In *Reality and the Vision,* a publication of the Chrysostom Society, a fellowship of "Christian authors," L'Engle identifies her beliefs with Joseph Campbell's "mythical view of the universe."[19] What is surprising is that this woman would protest loudly in one setting that she knows nothing about the New Age movement, while openly endorsing New Age proponents and philosophies in a different forum.

Spirit Guides

A few years ago, the concept of "spirit guides" would have been foreign to most people. Now, however, children are taught in their classrooms to conjure up these demons in their imaginations. The *Children's Literature Review* comments on the three spirit guides who escort Charles Wallace and Meg into another world of conflict in *A Wrinkle in Time.* What happens "occurs in a place beneath the level of consciousness . . . (an altered state of consciousness)," as the children "travel" with the aid of spiritual guides.[20]

L'Engle deceptively calls these creatures "guardian angels" and "messengers from God." However, these "angels" take the children in the story to a medium to gaze into her crystal ball and discover information they need to know in order to help their father. Could true believers ever think angels from God would escort children to a medium? Interestingly, many Christians we talked with had seen nothing strange about the idea. In fact, in discussing *A Wrinkle in Time*, one woman remarked that she could see nothing wrong in going to a medium as long as it was "for good." Nothing wrong? Have Christians been brainwashed to accept practices that God detests?

In Leviticus 20:6, God told Moses, "I will set my face against the person who turns to mediums and spiritists to prostitute himself by following them, and I will cut him off from his people." God equates witchcraft with spiritual prostitution, calling it "evil." I Samuel 15:23 tells us that "rebellion is as the sin of witchcraft." How did God react when Saul consulted with the medium at Endor? God took Saul's life!

Scripture makes it very clear that angels sent from Jehovah God would never escort children to a medium, for any reason.

The Plausible Impossible

On numerous occasions, L'Engle has been confronted about the promotion of occult practices in her works. She has been quick to gloss over the issues at hand with flippant answers. In her lecture "The Plausible Impossible," presented at Wheaton College, she was asked, "Do you believe that God abhors mediums, witchcraft, magic, and the like?" She replied, "Oh! You know, I wrote *Wrinkle in Time* in a more innocent world . . ." She continued by saying she knew nothing about the occult and proceeded to compare the biblical book of Revelation to a book of the occult. In answering the question, she excused herself by saying, "I made it clear that the medium never looked into the future." So what? The Bible—the Christian's handbook for life—warns us not to consult a medium.

Hundreds of people at Wheaton College laughed and applauded L'Engle's response to the questions by concerned Christians. The president of Trinity Christian College in Palos Heights, Illinois, and his wife were in attendance that night. His wife, who is librarian at Orland Park Christian Reformed Church, said L'Engle's books "minister to me as a Christian" and she added them to the church library. These books are also "recommended for use by students in children's literature and other education classes" at Trinity Christian College according to a letter reprinted 16 January 1990 from Mary Beth Bootsma to Orland Park's education committee.

Necromancy

During this same lecture at Wheaton, L'Engle personalized her belief in communicating with the dead by describing an encounter with her dead husband. She asked her audience, "Can those who are a part of that great cloud of witnesses which has gone before us be in two places at once? I believe that they can. . . ." She went on to tell of an incident that occurred after retiring one evening while on a small boat with her eldest daughter and her family.

She explained, "After awhile, I slid into 'wakefulness,' and I was aware that Hugh, my husband, was in bed with me, and it seemed perfectly natural that he be there. I was in that state which is neither waking nor dreaming, and I was grateful for his presence; though I knew that I must move very carefully and not touch him, because if I did, he would vanish. At the time that I was having this sense of Hugh's presence, around midnight or a little later, a radio call came through and Josephine and Alan heard it. I didn't. They went to the radio room, and they learned that Tallis had died."[21] Cannon Tallis was a priest at the Cathedral of St. John the Divine and a close friend of L'Engle and her family.

The next morning she asked her daughter (who was supposed to be "rational and eminently reasonable") if *she* thought her father had been there to tell her about the death of Tallis. Josephine replied, "Well, Mother, that thought had crossed my mind," and she laughed.

What Madeleine L'Engle accomplished at that lecture was to deliver the message that even the most rational, reasonable people believe in necromancy—communication with the dead. And the audience bought it! Christians need to see the subtle way this woman introduces biblically pronounced abominations into the Christian sector and makes them seem like the "plausible impossible."

The Triple Goddesses

Throughout pagan/occult history is the belief in a female trinity that takes on many different characters. In her book, *A Wrinkle in Time*, L'Engle introduces Mrs. Who, Mrs. Which, and Mrs. Whatsit. Just who or what are these weird creatures who lead L'Engle's Meg and Charles Wallace through time? While L'Engle claims they are angels, her literary critics equate them with witches and occult figures. The *Children's Literature Review* suggests that the "three-fold female figures are derived from the triple goddesses who abound in mythology, whether it's the three Fates, the three-faced Hecate, the triple fertility goddess of the ancient Near East, the trifold Morrigan or in a late incarnation as the three witches in Macbeth."[22]

The impact of *A Wrinkle in Time* was even felt in a Christian elementary school outside of Chicago. Teachers dressed up in costumes as Mrs. Which, Mrs. Who, and Mrs. Whatsit. The children had to guess which witch was which. While they were all having fun, they seemed to overlook the occult implications of L'Engle's book.

The *Concise Lexicon of the Occult* defines the "triple goddess" as "a Goddess trinity having three different aspects and three different names. The Moon Mother is worshipped as a Triple Goddess whose sacred symbol is the crescent moon. Her three goddess aspects correspond to the three lunar phases. In her waxing phase, she is the maiden. In her full moon phase she is the mother. In her waning or dark moon phase, she is the crone of wisdom, death and darkness." Interestingly, the descriptions of maiden, mother, and crone fit the descriptions of Mrs. Who, Mrs. Which, and Mrs. Whatsit.

In *Stone for a Pillow*, one of her non-fiction "Christian" books, feminist Madeleine L'Engle actually promotes the use of this symbol of paganism—the moon.

> In some early civilizations the crescent moon was a symbol of worship of the goddess Ishtar or Astaroth, and other female deities, like Diana, whose symbol was the moon. These goddesses were said to be beneficent when the moon was waxing, and maleficent when it was waning. In countries where the crops followed the phases of the moon, where earth was mother, the worship of the moon goddess was natural. . . . Perhaps the fear of the symbol of the crescent moon and the stars is a masculine fear of the feminine. But we need to regain the feminine, the intuitive, the nurturing element in ourselves, and in our understanding of the Godhead, our Maker, who is all in all, mother, father, brother, sister, lover, friend, companion. . . . Let us not be bullied into fearing the feminine symbol of the crescent moon.[23]

But were these pagan goddesses really benign, loving deities that lived in compatible co-existence with God, as L'Engle attempts to portray? And if so, why did God condemn their worship as detestable in his sight?

The commentary from the NIV Study Bible explains who both Astoreth and Ishtar were

> female deities such as Astoreth (consort of Baal) and Asherah (consort of El, the chief god of the Canaanite pantheon). . . . Ashtoreth was associated with the evening star and was the beautiful goddess of war and fertility. She was worshipped as Ishtar in Babylonia and as Athtart in Aram. To the Greeks she was Astarte or Aphrodite, and to the Romans, Venus. Worship of the Ashtoreths involved extremely lascivious practices.[24]

The worship of these false gods was not holy and uplifting but was instead totally debased. High groves of trees surrounded temples in which male, female, and homosexual prostitution was conducted in the name of the deities. Even more heinous practices that took place during that time included the burning alive of infant offspring in fires that glowed within the bellies of the idols.

L'Engle cannot believe that a loving God would punish the people who conducted such practices? God knows that perversion begets perversion. In the disobedience to His command to destroy all remnants of pagan beliefs, the people of Israel turned to evil ways and incurred God's wrath.

> They also set up for themselves high places, sacred stones and Asherah poles on every high hill and under every spreading tree. There were even male shrine prostitutes in the land; the people engaged in all the detestable practices of the nations the Lord had driven out before the Israelites. (I Kings 14:23-24)

Remember what L'Engle said about the "tribal" god who drove out the nations before the Israelites? Why would a "Christian" continually deny God's condemnation of such hideous practices?

Feminism

Madeleine L'Engle is a self-proclaimed feminist. Throughout her writings she venomously mocks the male gender of God. In her book, *The Irrational Season*, she describes Him as "the paternalistic male chauvinist pig Old Testament God. . . ."[25] This is Almighty God, the Father of Jesus Christ, that she is speaking about!

Feminists in the churches, who themselves have just as much difficulty with God's male classification, tend to feed on such books. In 1987, L'Engle wrote an article on feminist spirituality for *Ms. Magazine*. In it she talked about the triumph of women being ordained in the churches and finally "that these women are given the opportunity to free the churches and temples from a narrow vision of creation and our place in it, and that they may reveal a Creator who is. . . . exquisite." She continues, "How many people visualize God as looking like Moses—long beard, white nightgown—and Moses in a bad temper, at that? Male, Chauvinist. Punitive. I want a Creator who is exquisite."[26]

What is this woman saying? Does she fear God or His Word? In Proverbs 1:7 we read, "The fear of the Lord is the beginning of knowledge, but fools despise wisdom and discipline."

The feminist movement is spreading throughout the Church with incredible fervor—Madeleine L'Engle being one of the leading influences. Those who are praying, "Our Mother who art . . ." are actually returning to pagan goddess worship. If people only knew what was underneath this ungodly, feminist perversion of Scripture, they would call the Church into account. God will Himself, someday.

Naming and the Named

While L'Engle's primer, *A Wrinkle in Time*, introduces children to the world of the occult, *A Wind in the Door* takes young readers a step further. In the first book, the children meet "angels" who shape-change into "centaurs" (half animal/half human creatures), consult mediums, execute astral travel, and use mental telepathy. L'Engle calls these spirit-guides "guardian angels from God," but they seem nothing more than demons in disguise, contacted and invoked by the use of occult techniques and meditation. Then we found that *A Wind in the Door* makes *Wrinkle* seem mild.

In *Wind,* the occult overtones are far more blatant. The children are approached by a "cherubim," described by Charles Wallace as "a fierce, wild being"—a dragon. Then, a tall, dark form dressed in a dark, hooded robe appears and introduces himself to the children as a "Teacher." This Teacher, who is named Blajeny, informs Charles and Meg of three ordeals that they must endure. He then leaves them to accomplish these tasks with the help of Progo, the "cherubim," and occult powers. The Teacher Blajeny reappears occasionally to take them to their next ordeal.

It is here that L'Engle introduces something called "the naming and the named" as a practice. In fact, *Wind* is a handbook for this occult art, though the concept appears in many of L'Engle's books. *Revision*, a New Age/occult magazine, defines "the naming and the named" as the "calling down of the Spirit" . . . to give power and life to whatever has been "named." Essentially, this is a ritual and could be assessed as an open invitation to demon possession. In the end of the book, that is exactly how this "gift" is used.

Throughout *Wind*, the Teacher and Progo carefully train the children in occult practices. At one point Blajeny shows reverence to the children's black pet snake, Louise the Larger, by bowing down to her and proclaiming that she is also a Teacher. L'Engle carefully paints the snake as wise, affectionate, loving, and with "impeccable judgment about human nature."

The cherubim, who takes the physical shape of the pagan Egyptian version of a cherubim, has an amulet eye by which he pulls Meg out of her body and *through* his eye. In this way, she can stand on ground that does not exist, except of course in the imagination of the Teacher. (This is known as the "Mind's Eye.") She eventually enters the human cells of the body of her critically ill brother to heal him—a form of shamanism.

(Teaching people that they can shrink themselves through visualization is not uncommon among New Age curriculum developers. During a teacher recertification course in Colorado, instructional information was handed out to the attendees for a guided imagery "trip" into a strawberry, for the purpose of "studying" it from the inside. The teachers were told that they could heal themselves, simply by using this same process of visualization—the one that Meg uses in the story.)

Meg has been told that she is a "Namer" and that she must learn to employ this "gift" while inside of her brother in order to empower her companions and defeat the Echthroi, or fallen angels (demons), who are killing her brother. Through the practice of "naming," she can empower, change, and redeem others, human or spirit. Meg struggles at first, but, in the end, she "names" the demons, embracing them, and taking them into herself. In this way, she has supposedly redeemed them, and, of course, her brother is healed. But God is not going to redeem the demons! We are to resist the devil, not invite him in for tea. Demonic possession doesn't heal; it destroys.

The ever-so-helpful cherubim also teaches Meg the art of "kything." At one point, Progo (which means "to know" psychically) tells Meg she must open her mind. "'Your conscious mind doesn't have the key to the storehouse. All I want you to do is open yourself up to me so that I can open the door to your mind's storehouse.'"[27]

Further along, Progo again attempts to probe Meg's mind. "'Stop blocking me. It's our only hope. You must let me kythe with you.' She felt him moving about within her mind, more gently now, but persistently. 'You're still blocking me . . . let me in,'" he says.[28]

Because L'Engle continually stresses the importance of "naming," claiming that by naming someone or something, you empower or give life to that person or thing, we decided to investigate the unusual *names* she has chosen for her characters. What we found was most revealing. Many of these names are actually names of demons and pagan deities! In fact, "Blajeny" is the Hindu god of the dead, the overlord of all that is dark and evil! Blajeny is the Hindu Satan. In the story, he has been chosen to teach Charles Wallace, the "new" human, the "aquarian man."

Why does a professing Christian give demonic names to her characters? She repeatedly states that her books have a life of their own, that they often become true. Is she trying to give life to these demonic forces and pagan gods by naming them in her books?

Very interesting, isn't it? These books are not unfamiliar to our children. They have been placed in many public and private schools and libraries throughout the country. Christian schools have them, as well. They indoctrinate our children into New Age/occult mysticism.

L'Engle's books introduce school children in the classroom to shimmery, light-filled "spiritguides," sometimes referred to by the teachers as "guardian angels."

Madeleine L'Engle's fantasy novels assure children that it is all right to open their minds to the control of spirit beings, teachers, or whatever chooses to come in. L'Engle is presenting a highly dangerous and seductive message to the young and old alike. Our society has been bombarded and fascinated with occult messages, and we will all pay an awful price by allowing our children to be introduced to the supernatural world of demons. Allowing a "spirit" to empower anyone is an open invitation to possession.

It's no wonder the Teacher Blajeny bowed down to the snake! Revelation 12:9b states: ". . . that ancient serpent called the devil or Satan, who leads the whole world astray . . . he was hurled to the earth and his angels with him."

Parents need to check the required reading lists of their children's schools. And, they need to ask their children specifically if they've read Madeleine L'Engle's books. Peruse their reading sources. Many school libraries and numerous Christian church and school libraries promote her books.

A Wind in the Door is a very scary book. Beware, for the sake of your children. Know that an ongoing familiarity with the occult could take its toll.

Runes

In *A Swiftly Tilting Planet*, the last book of the *Time Trilogy*, L'Engle comes out of the closet and actually uses the correct names for some of the occult techniques that had not yet been introduced into the trilogy.

Magical runes are employed by Charles Wallace to help him in time of need. "Rune" literally means "secret." Originating with the Northern Europeans, runes once referred to anything secret, but came to mean lines of written magic spells. L'Engle has blatantly referred to runes and their use in every chapter. Cleverly, she also uses the chapter titles to make up a rune, which we found in *Celtic Christianity*, published by Lindisfarne Press (see chapter 5.). One could say, the whole book is a rune.

In the occult book, *A Magical Language of Runes*, author P.M.H. Atwater states,

> No matter what mythology you read from . . . there is reference after reference given to runes: runes everlasting, runes life giving, runes as magic signs, runes to invoke the gods and spirit keepers. Never does anyone simply say, 'I know my alphabet letters.' Rather, they go on and on about how well versed they are in rune spells for any crisis, need condition or purpose. . . . Runes always remain first and foremost a magical language of sacred thoughts and secret deeds.[29]

What we find so horrendous in this book is the way L'Engle twists evil for good. Charles Wallace, going back in time in his quest to change the future, jumps in and out of bodies (kything). In his travels, Charles "becomes" Brandon, a son of early settlers during the time of the Salem witch trials. (In an apparent attempt to discredit the godly people who founded our country, L'Engle refers to these settlers as "Pilgrims," although the witch trials actually occurred after the time of the true Pilgrims. Remember, though, L'Engle doesn't get hung up on chronology, as she repeatedly says.)

In her book, the pagan Indians and those who are tolerant of occult beliefs are painted as "godly" people. The others, particularly the pastor, are presented as hateful, lying, bigoted witch-hunters who anger God.

In L'Engle's book, the pastor, who is portrayed as an idiotic, evil, lustful man, accuses an Indian girl of witchcraft and sentences her to death by hanging, leaving the girl's newborn infant motherless. As she is led up the steps to the gallows, Charles Wallace uses a rune to call down "power" from heaven. In response to his call, thunderstorms come, and lightning strikes the church, setting it on fire. Lightning strikes again, sending the pastor sprawling on the ground, his arm burned.

Throughout this book, magical runes and Indian gods provide infinite help, as do "kything" and "tessering." In all of L'Engle's works, there is a compatibility and even friendly coexistence between God and the pagan deities. When the Indian woman was questioned about her religion, she claimed there was no difference between her pagan beliefs and the teachings of Jesus Christ.[30] What L'Engle succeeds in doing is to portray Christians as evil and those who practice paganism as good.

Scrying

Another occult practice prevalent in L'Engle's book, *A Swiftly Tilting Planet*, is scrying. Scott Cunningham, a practicing witch himself, wrote *The Truth about Witchcraft Today*, in which he defines scrying:

> To gaze at or into an object (a quartz crystal, sphere, pool of water, reflections, a candle flame) to still the Conscious Mind in order to contact the Psychic Mind. This practice allows the scryer to become aware of events prior to their actual occurrence, as well as to perceive past or present events through other than the five senses. A form of divination.[31]

In his journey through time, the character Charles Wallace uses a pool of water, a metal sphere, and "a scrying glass" to receive pictures of the future. His ability to do this is called "second sight," another term for "clairvoyance." L'Engle describes his psychic ability as "God's gift."[32]

There is certainly no difference between Charles Wallace's strange and unusual "gift" and the spirit of fortune-telling, which possessed a slave girl in the ancient city of Philippi. The girl had badgered the apostle Paul and others until "he turned around and said to the spirit, 'In the name of Jesus Christ I command you to come out of her!' At that moment the spirit left her" (Acts 16:18).

CHAPTER TWO

OOOOOOOOOOOOOOOOOOOOOOOOOOOOOOOOOOOOOOOOOOOOOO

OCCULT 102

Fantasy World

According to her writings, Madeleine L'Engle was born in New York on 29 November 1918, the daughter of Charles Wadsworth Camp (a foreign correspondent, distinguished naturalist, and drama and music critic) and Madeleine Camp, an accomplished pianist. An only child, she was brought up in the formal English tradition her father wished, with a nanny and governess. Their upper-middle-class home bustled with the artsy and the intellectual—a peculiar slice of people. Madeleine used to sneak downstairs late in the evening, hide under the piano, and listen to their conversations long after her bedtime.

Her father had been gassed in World War I. As his physical health deteriorated, his professional work also suffered. His lungs became so afflicted that he could no longer live in New York or any of the other cosmopolitan cities he loved. The family moved to Switzerland, and L'Engle went to the first of a series of boarding schools, both in Europe and in the United States. L'Engle graduated from Smith College with honors and did graduate work at Columbia University. She pursued a career in the theater for the next five years, because she thought it would be good schooling for a writer.[1]

A sheltered young girl growing up in New York City, L'Engle lived much of her early years in solitude, even taking her meals alone and enjoying her solitude.

Somewhat lame, with one leg slightly shorter than the other and having quite an active imagination, the child Madeleine turned inward to a world of fantasy, filled her mind with books, and made up her own stories. She wrote her first book, she says, at age six "about a little 'grul' who lived in a cloud."[2]

In her fourth, fifth, and sixth grades, she says her awkwardness became a point of ridicule for other students and her homeroom teacher. L'Engle felt they interpreted her lack of ability to perform well in sports to mean that she wasn't very smart, either. She buried herself even deeper in her "interior" mind. This was the place where she would escape to, and she began to see it as the "real world."

Levitation

As a small child, L'Engle was able to "float" down the spiral stairs at her grandmother's house. She'd walk up the stairs and just float down without touching, an accomplishment she called "a special joy to me." Floating happens to be a form of levitation, which is performed while in a semi-trance or full-trance and is, according to the *Psychic Encyclopedic Dictionary*, "always willed" and "desire-controlled." It is "accomplished by the undivided concentration of the subconscious mind and by the [spirit] guides."[3]

L'Engle reports,

> I think I went up the regular way, but I came down without touching. Perhaps it was because I was so used to thinking things over in solitude that it never occurred to me to tell anybody about this marvelous thing, and because I never told it, nobody told me it was impossible.[4]

She learned early on how to go into a trance, to tap into her subconscious. She writes about a certain part of her mind, her "creative unconscious" (also known as the "collective unconscious"), being the place where she stored up all that she saw, heard, smelled, and tasted. It is from this "complete sensory recollection" that she claims to write her stories.

Meeting the Heavens

L'Engle shares a strange incident that happened to her as an infant, where some people (she doesn't tell us who) carried her down to the beach in the middle of the night to introduce her to the stars and the universe. She says:

> One of the most important things that ever happened to me was when I was a very, very small child, visiting my grandmother at her beach cottage in North Florida. And it must have been an extraordinarily beautiful night for someone to say, "Let's wake up the baby and show her the stars." I was picked up and carried downstairs and onto the beach. And there were the stars in all their glory and that was my first glimpse of night and my first glimpse of the numinous world and my first awareness of the enormity and depth and excitement of the Universe. Now, all of this was obviously NOT CONSCIOUS, but the fact that that is so strong a memory that it is reawakened every time I see the stars, it's made a difference as to how I've thought about *everything* all of my life.[5]

Later in her life, she found a favorite spot, about five minutes from her home in Connecticut, where she could do her "Zen method of contemplation." It was a large rock that she sprawls across to gaze at the stars and to ponder her role as a co-creator of the universe. "One of my most-loved places for this kind of prayer is a large glacial rock on which I stretch out, flat on my back, so that I can feel that I am part of the turning of the planet, so that rock and I merge, *becoming part of the energy of creation*"[6] (emphasis added).

To Europe

Through the years, L'Engle's illness-stricken, family life took many sad and chaotic turns. As her father's condition worsened, they sought a place where he could breathe more comfortably. The family rented a chateau in the French Alps, where they spent a summer. Not unusual for Madeleine, she submerged during that time into the sub-recesses of her mind.

She wrote,

> I was happy that summer because I lived *completely in the world of the imagination*—the only way I could escape being drawn into my parents' unhappiness. I wandered through the centuries, being the daughter of the chateau, Madeleine in the twelfth century, the fifteenth, the eighteenth. I wrote stories and poems, and I lived an *interior life* which protected me from the teasing of the three boys as well as from the world of the grown-ups.[7] (emphasis added)

L'Engle was sent off to a Swiss boarding school, where she was the only American. She was even lonelier than before; the school was rigid, and the new surroundings stifled her. She began having difficulty with her "imaginary world" and looked for ways to reawaken it. The girls at the school were each given a number—her's was 97—"even then, the process of un-Naming had begun"[8] (see chapter 1).

Poppy Seed Dreams

As a school project, the students were assigned little plots of ground where they were to grow their own gardens for produce for tea time . . . watercress, lettuce, tomatoes, radishes, and so forth. However, L'Engle and her partner (number 96) decided to plant only poppies, because they knew from their "illicit reading" that opium comes from poppies and that opium produces "beautiful dreams."[9]

So, the girls "ate poppy-seed sandwiches, poppy-flower sandwiches, poppy-leaf sandwiches, and went to bed every night with our dream books and flashlights under our pillows."[10] They soon discovered they didn't need poppy sandwiches to induce dreams, but for them, the poppy seeds opened up a new "awareness" to another world.

Thus L'Engle began her lucid dream experiments and later became a student of Carl Jung's "dream analysis." Throughout her books, she maintains that *dreams are far more real than is consciousness.* And, to this day, she cherishes her bedtime, when she enters the world of the imagination and moves into the "infinite mind."[11]

Lucid Dreams

According to dream theorists and occultists, "lucid dreams are dreams in which the dreamer is aware that he is dreaming while he is dreaming."[12] The dreamer experiences something called "the onset of lucidity." This shift of consciousness is sometimes described as bursting out of the clouds in an airplane flight and feeling dazzled by the clear sunlight.

Some dreamers report experiencing a feeling of "energies" moving about in the body and mind, leaving a tingly sensation that is often accompanied by gorgeous, vivid colors, intense and ecstatic feelings, or celestial music that seems to come from another world. It is definitely a head trip, nudged along by demonic activity and sometimes drugs.

Madeleine Grows Up

As a young woman, Madeleine L'Engle landed work in a New York theater, where she met her husband-to-be, handsome actor Hugh Franklin. She wrote two novels backstage in a dressing room waiting for her entrances. She loved the theater experience, where she says she developed friendships that have lasted even beyond death.[13] She'd known early on that she wanted to write more than act, and felt always that she had been "called" to write. She married Hugh Franklin, and they left the theater and moved to Connecticut, where they maintained a two hundred-year-old house and shared in the running of a general store for about nine years. Later, Hugh Franklin became well-known for his role as Dr. Tyler in the TV soap "All My Children."

She continued writing, even while mothering their three children, Josephine, Maria, and Bion. She was able to "keep the world out" by invoking a "force field" of silence around herself where she could go on writing her stories and her poems and dreaming her dreams. She could write anywhere, on planes, in hotels. The force field was interrupted only by crawling babies. (Force fields, or "energy fields," are known as "electrical auras," commonly used by psychics for protection and intelligence.)

While her children grew up (Josephine married Alan Jones, the Episcopalian minister of Grace Cathedral in San Francisco, which is promoted in the *New Age Journal*), L'Engle received numerous awards for her large volume of work. Some of these include: John Newbery Medal, 1963; runner-up for the Hans Christian Andersen Award, 1964; Sequoia Award, 1965; Lewis Carroll Shelf, 1965—all for *A Wrinkle in Time*; Austrian State Prize, 1979, for *The Moon by Night*; University of Mississippi Medallion, 1978, and American Book Award, 1980, for *A Swiftly Tilting Planet*; Newbery Honor Book Award, 1981, for *A Ring of Endless Light*; and the Catholic Library Association's Regina Award, given for consistent, sustained quality of work . . . to name a few. She's been named on the "top ten" most popular authors lists in *American Bookseller*, and in *Publisher's Weekly* as one of the top six.

A Servant of the Work

L'Engle is author-in-residence at the New Age Gothic Cathedral of St. John the Divine in New York, where she occasionally gives sermons. It is there that she can get away to her own office and just "write." She believes she has been chosen by a "Higher Power," that her work is "God's gift." She even held her Bible in her hands in an act of dedication to her "Maker," that she might write in order "to serve the Word."

In so serving the Word, she claims that she doesn't really write the books at all. Rather, they are written through her. She gets out of the way, and it just comes. She dramatically states that she surrenders to "the work." She serves "the books," which she claims "take on a life of their own." If indeed words coming through her computer are "taking on a life of their own," and are "alive," then is she comparing her writings to the Holy Scriptures?

The Bible describes itself as follows: "The word of God is living and active. Sharper than any double-edged sword, it penetrates even to dividing soul and spirit, joints and marrow; it judges the thoughts and attitudes of the heart" (Heb. 4:12).

In her book, *Walking on Water*, L'Engle writes, "To serve a work of art is almost identical with adoring the Master of the Universe in contemplative prayer."[14]

When L'Engle delivered her October 1989 "Christians Keeping Faith in the New Age" talk to an audience at Cherry Hills Community Church in Denver, she said, "I don't choose the books I'm going to write. They are given to me, and I have to do the best I can with them."* Often, she asserts that she doesn't understand the books until a few years later, after they are published. We find these statements to be both arrogant and contradictory, since she confesses that she often has to rewrite them several times. That being the case, it is obvious that the higher power to which she attributes her books didn't get it right the first time around.

Confronting the Issue

Although some have never heard of the woman, L'Engle is well-known in literary circles, many of our churches and Christian schools, and, of course, in the New Age movement. Her works are included in many mandatory reading programs within the education system. In fact, she has an almost cult-like following.

---

*Since L'Engle claims to know nothing about the New Age, it seems strange that she should choose this topic for her speech. In her speech, she defined the New Age as coming "into being 2,000 years ago, when Jesus Christ came to live with us, to show us what it means to be a human being." But mankind already knew how to be human beings; that was the problem. Jesus came to set us free from our sinful nature and spiritual death caused by our being human, the descendants of Adam.

We found her books at the Theosophical Society's Quest Bookstore in Wheaton, Illinois, which confirmed our conclusions regarding their content. Unfortunately, we also found them in many Christian bookstores as well, including a well-known Christian bookstore in Denver, Colorado.

In spite of what she says to the contrary, Madeleine L'Engle's writings do contain, promote, and teach a whole gamut of New Age topics, philosophies, and techniques, including, but not limited to: magic, divination, spirit guides, crystal balls, mediums, fortune telling, spells, monism, pantheism, nature worship, Zen meditation, lesbianism, graphic fornication, cosmic consciousness, druids, human sacrifice, demons, dragons, runes, divination, astral travel, and on and on.

These are all elements of the occult, which she has put in a box and marked "For Children."

Altered States of Consciousness (ASCs)

Madeleine L'Engle lives in a world slightly different from most people who profess to be Christians. However, her experiences are quite common to occultists and could be considered the norm for esoterists. The following personal account is from her book, *And It Was Good*, part of the Wheaton Literary Series published by Harold Shaw Publishers:

> I ambled down the lane, pausing to pick flowers as I saw them, daisies, buttercups, and my mind happily drifted with the breeze. And I was not thinking at all. And then I moved, was moved, into what I supposed would be called an *altered state of being*. It is, when it happens, a far deeper state of being than the one we live in normally. Everything is more real. . . .[15] (emphasis added)

New Agers and occultists see their world through violet-colored glasses (violet, being the official color for the New Age movement) and altered states of consciousness. For them, it is in the self-induced or drug-induced states of "being" where their view of reality is developed.

Trancing is not conducive to reasoning or sound judgment about anything. It is in trances that New Agers call forth and meet their spirit guides and their "guardian angels." It is in trances that they write their books, their music, and their poetry.

Co-creators

In the foreword of *And It Was Good*, Luci Shaw, a former member of the English staff at Wheaton College, writes:

> For years, a persistent and hitherto unsolved question of mine has been, "Who was the poet of Genesis?" . . . I think Madeleine L'Engle has given me an answer. In developing her concept of *co-creativity* and *co-creators* she helps me to see how it is possible for God and man to work together—the primal impulse of God as Maker, First Poet of the universe . . . *inspiriting, ingodding human thinking and imagination* until the divine world becomes enfleshed and is expressed in human language.[16]

Shaw continues:

> As we worked together through the intricacies of the manuscript of *And It Was Good*, time and time again I literally caught my breath at some of Madeleine's outrageous statements. "Madeleine, you *can't say* that!" I would explode, protesting the radical nature of her declarations. . . . But reading further, penetrating deeper, I would grasp the holy logic of her conclusions and find myself acknowledging, "You not only *can* say that, you *should!*"[17]

Luci Shaw endorsed the New Age concept of "co-creation" in L'Engle's book, along with the rest of its heresies. Of course, her endorsement promotes the book on a very large scale. In fact, Wheaton College, the "Harvard of the Evangelicals," supports L'Engle so enthusiastically that she refers to the institution as her second home.[18]

L'Engle goes on in her book, "God created, and it was joy: time, space, matter. There is and we are part of that is-ness, part of that becoming. That is our calling: co-creation. Every single one of us, without exception, is called to co-create with God."[19] "If we accept that God is within each of us, then God will give us, within us, the courage to accept the responsibility of being co-creators." She's talking about being "gods."

Co-creators? Are we equal to God? Does He need our help to create? Our question to L'Engle is this: *WHERE WERE YOU* when God laid the foundations of the world? God Himself asks:

> Tell me, if you understand. Who marked off its dimensions? Surely you know! Who stretched a measuring line across it? On what were its footings set, or who laid its cornerstone—while the morning stars sang together and all angels shouted for joy? Who shut up the sea behind its doors when it burst forth from the womb, when I made the clouds its garment and wrapped it in thick darkness, when I fixed limits for it and set its doors and bars in place, when I said "This far you may come and no farther; here is where your proud waves halt"?
>
> Have you ever given orders to the morning or shown the dawn its place. . . . Have you journeyed to the springs of the sea or walked in the recesses of the deep? Have the gates of death been shown to you? Have you comprehended the vast expanses of the earth? Tell me, if you know all this. . . .
>
> Have you entered the storehouses of the snow or seen the storehouses of hail. . . . What is the way to the place where the lightning is dispersed or the place where the east winds are scattered over the earth?
>
> Can you bind the beautiful Pleiades? Can you loose the cords of Orion? Can you bring forth the constellations in their seasons or lead out the Bear with its cubs? Do you know the laws of the heav-

ens? Can you set up God's dominion over the earth?
(Job 38: 4-12, 16-18, 22, 24, 31-33)

The Bible answers with a resounding *NO!* "Know ye
that the Lord He is God. *It is He who hath made us and
not we ourselves*" (Ps. 100:3a).

Brain Waves

L'Engle's brand of religion relies heavily on changing
brain wave patterns by something called "spiritual disciplines," which include yoga, meditation, self-hypnosis,
biofeedback, visualization, imagery, relaxation exercises,
chanting mantras, etc. Altered states then open the door
to the subconscious mind, part of the "Universal Mind."

However, God, in His infinite wisdom, created us
with strange and wonderful brains. All day long, our
brain wave patterns change, normally and naturally. In
fact, fluctuation in the electrical activity of the brain can
be recorded with an electro-encephalograph (EEG). These
are categorized in four fundamental frequency ranges:
beta, alpha, theta, and delta. *Beta* waves are dominant
during periods of wakefulness, activity, decision-making
and strong sensory perception. *Alpha* waves are associated with light to medium states of relaxation, *theta*
more with sleep, and *delta* waves dominate during deep
sleep.

Tampered Minds

There is a movement afoot, however, that is tamper-
ing with these other-wise normal brain waves. New Age
advocates are training folks to interrupt and short-cir-
cuit people's minds through stress management, relaxation, and self-help programs. These programs teach
participants techniques to aid in inducing trance at the
alpha level and sometimes at an even deeper state.

No one seems to be exempt from the exercise that
begins, "Relax, take a few deep breaths, clear your minds."
Or to relaxation tapes for use in the car or with head-
phones. Students, soldiers, businessmen, pilots, church

members, athletes, nurses, senior citizens . . . most of society has been taught to go into "euphoric" altered states.

Even more frightening is the fact that people are going into trances while they are *supposed* to be awake. They are walking around, driving cars, teaching our children, operating military equipment. We even see them in churches after lengthy praise and worship services.

People seem to be looking for "stress control" and emotional and spiritual "highs." What they are getting is an endorphin rush, a sort of "runner's high." The furthest thing from their minds is a possible encounter with a demon through this open door. It is a trendy practice closing down people's judgment yet opening them up to whoever—or whatever—wants to control their minds.

When it comes to the resulting capacities, there is basically no difference between drinking-and-driving and meditating-and-driving. They can both be hazardous, though only one is considered to be illegal.

Witches Do It

When witches gather in covens, they use certain rituals for creating altered states of mind and for practicing magic. Miriam Starhawk, who calls herself a goddess-worshipping pagan witch, has written a book called *Spiral Dance* in which she gives the four basic skills every young witch needs to master for magic. Those skills are: 1) relaxation, 2) concentration, 3) visualization, and 4) projection or manifestation. It is interesting that L'Engle teaches these same four steps in her books.

Relaxing the body, clearing the mind and concentrating on the breath or chanting a sound, visualizing a wish, setting the picture in the mind and then projecting it into reality—that's magic. Occultists learn to astral project in the mind, until they believe they actually do the very thing they are visualizing. Amazingly, more than half of the people in our country have been taught these skills. Thousands of children are learning them every day in their public and private schools.

Churches Not Exempt

Repetitive phrases, lengthy periods of emotional worship, visualization, and something called "contemplative prayer" can be trance-inducing as well. The Church needs to be warned. One pastor told us he was in a worship service and suddenly felt he had left his body, floating above the congregation. Unfortunately, this particular pastor thought this was a great experience. Christians need to be sober-minded and that includes being able to think and pray, to listen and communicate, and to discern good from evil.

Jesus told us, "And when you pray, do not keep on babbling like pagans, for they think they will be heard because of their many words. Do not be like them, for your Father knows what you need before you ask him" (Matt. 6:7-8).

The Apostle Peter knew the benefit of staying alert, having himself been rebuked and humbled by Jesus for falling asleep on the job. Peter warned, "The end of all things is near. Therefore be clear minded and self-controlled so that you can pray" (I Pet. 4:7).

CHAPTER THREE

○○

Jesus Christ: A Druid?

Do you want to be a peacemaker? Are you willing to risk your life to end wars? Do you wish to possess the "ancient wisdoms," to know the meaning of the stars, to understand the language of Eden? Would you like to have the gift of healing, not just human ills, but the woes of the planet as well? Do you want to be like Christ?

Then join the Druids! This is the potent message of Madeleine L'Engle's recent novel, *An Acceptable Time.* In this book, Polly (daughter of Meg and Calvin from the *Time Trilogy*) has gone to her grandparents' home to study. It is Samhain, or Halloween, a time when Druids and witches believe "the veil between the worlds was thinnest and the dead could be contacted for help and knowledge."[1]

Because of this magical setting, the Druids are able to come into the present, and Polly catches a glimpse of them at the famous glacial rock. Another pathway to the past is her grandparents' swimming pool, which was built over a sacred druid pond. Polly and the Episcopalian priest, Bishop Colubra (*colubra* meaning snake, an appropriate title in this instance), travel back three thousand years, and the adventures—and misinformation—begin.

The Evidence

"Fortunately, not much is known about Druids," L'Engle told a laughing audience at Bethany Lutheran Church in Englewood, Colorado. We listened sadly as, encouraged by their cheers, she regaled them with readings from *An Acceptable Time*, her intriguing tale promoting the "holy" worship of druidism. She used this platform to criticize Christians for putting "God in a box" by teaching that salvation is in Christ alone, and she reiterated her theme that all paths lead to God.[2]

But the assertion that there is little or no evidence regarding druidic beliefs and practices is incorrect. Madeleine L'Engle claims to have done extensive research on this subject, so she should know better. There is, in fact, a great deal known about the Celts and their religion.

Druids were the priests of the ancient Celts in pre-Roman Gaul and Britain. These men and women were highly educated and literate, yet their "sacred teachings" were transmitted orally. This is not uncommon, however, with satanic cults. Not until Hitler did satanists keep detailed records.

The oral tradition of the Celts left many legends and customs, which give glimpses of the past. And though the Druids themselves didn't leave written records, other people did. Julius Caesar and the Greeks wrote extensively about the Celtic practices and beliefs, having had personal contacts with their priests. In addition, there were at least twelve other eyewitnesses who recorded the horrors of this evil religion. Additional evidence is also available through archaeological discoveries of statues, idols, engravings, and motifs on vessels found at temple sites.

And last, but certainly not least, are the bodies of murdered victims, incredibly preserved in the bogs in Great Britain.

So we *have* witnesses, physical evidence, and bodies. That's enough to bring in a murder conviction in any court of law.

The Role of the Druids

The Druids held a highly exalted position in society. They believed themselves to be above the rulers, and the majority of them had indeed been recruited from the noble class. In Ireland, even a king was not allowed to speak in the presence of a Druid unless the priest spoke first.

Druids performed three main functions. The first was to be a living repository of all the tribal knowledge regarding history, gods, and ceremonies. Because none of this information was recorded, Druids were the logical choice to be tutors among the nobility, which made it easy for them to select initiates. Training for the priesthood began between the ages of six and eight and lasted twenty years.[3] Like the Nazi SS, only the brightest people, and only those with no physical or mental blemishes, qualified.

Among the upper classes, at least, parents were not even allowed to name their own children. Instead, a temporary name would be given to them by a Druid at birth. A permanent name would either be earned or granted upon initiation.[4] It was also common to take children away from their homes and place them with foster parents, thus giving the priests more freedom from possible parental interference.

There is even evidence that some of the victims were raised for the sole purpose of becoming "divine sacrifices." (Such was probably the case of the Lindow Man, a murdered Druid prince whose perfectly preserved body was found in 1984.[5]) These people would be brainwashed from childhood to accept their execution willingly, believing that their death would ensure prosperity for their people and would be rewarded with a quick reincarnation.

Druids also served as judges over all civil and military matters. And how did they execute this power? Madeleine L'Engle portrays them as peacemakers to be emulated by all:

> Oh, listen, Grand, I like this. Before a battle, druids would often throw themselves between two armies to stop the war and bring peace . . . "They were peacemakers, then," her grandmother said. "I like that" . . . "Later on, after the Roman Empire took over, druids and Christians didn't get along.

Each appeared to be a threat to the other. I wonder if they really were. "Even Christians are threats
to each other," her grandmother said . . . "Wouldn't
it be great," Polly suggested, "If there were druids
to throw themselves between the battle lines of
Muslims and Christians and Palestinians and Jews
in the Middle East, or Catholics and Protestants in
Ireland."[6]

This portrait strays from the truth, however. Druids
did have the authority to stop wars and negotiate peace,
but then they were the ones who declared the wars in
the first place. And they were always on the sideline to
cast spells and perform witchcraft to aid their side.

Their authority in civil matters was greatly enhanced
by their power to excommunicate anyone who disagreed
with them. The poor soul who stood up against a Druid
lost all legal and religious rights. It has even been suggested that such a person stood in danger of becoming
the next sacrifice![7]

Perhaps the most important function of the Druids
was the performance of all religious activities, including
divination, astrology, witchcraft, and human and animal
sacrifice.

Human Sacrifice

Throughout her book, Madeleine L'Engle downplays
the Druid's practice of human sacrifice, presenting it as
an infrequent occurrence performed occasionally by a
heretical fringe. "Mrs. Murray asked, 'Was blood sacrifice part of the druidic ritual?' 'It's not been proven,'" the
"bishop" responds.[8] Nothing could be further from the
truth. Even Gwenc'hlan Le Scouezec, the current Great
Druid of Brittany, admits these murders occurred.[9]

The historical evidence is overwhelming. "Tacticus
alludes to the fact that the Druids of Anglesea 'covered
their alters with the blood of captives.'" Julius Caesar
wrote that human sacrifice was a common and frequent
occurrence among the Celts and that the Druids orches-
trated the carnage. When an army went to war, they
would often seek the gods' assistance with human sacri-

fice and pledge all of their captured booty to the gods in return for victory. If they won, they would build large wicker cages shaped like men. In these they would place all of the men, women, children, and animals taken in the battle and set them on fire in one large holocaust. It also appears that these mass murders occurred regularly at the feast of Beltain (1 May) to ensure fertility of the soil.[10] After harvest time, some druidic priests would burn the harvest foreman as a thanksgiving offering. (It's hard to imagine that there would be many applicants for that position!)

Stuart Piggott, a respected archaeologist and recognized authority on Celtic history, agrees:

> It is hardly realistic to exculpate the Druids from participation, probably active, in both the beliefs and practices involved in human sacrifice (which after all had only been brought to an end in the civilized Roman world in the early first century B.C.) The Druids were the wise men of barbarian Celtic society, and Celtic religion was their religion, with all its crudities. It is sheer romanticism and a capitulation to the myth of the Noble Savage to imagine that they stood by the sacrifices duty bound, but with disapproval on their faces and elevated thoughts in their minds.[11]

Sacrifice also accompanied the funerals of important people. One example of this was the burial of the Irish leader Fiachin—fifty hostages were entombed alive while the Druids sang the death-dirge.[12] "Divine sacrifices" were performed occasionally to guarantee the continued fertility of the land and in times of great crisis. "Lindow Man," the murdered Druid prince, was killed in A.D. 60 after the disastrous Roman conquests.[13] Dr. Anne Ross, another respected archaeologist and expert on the Celts, recounts other occasions when these slaughters occurred:

> Oran (Odran), one of [Saint] Columba's brethren seems to have been sacrificed when the foundations of the monastery [in Iona] were laid. . . . Welsh legend has it that a similar sacrifice was

recommended by the Druids during the building of Vortigern's castle. . . . The Druids ordered that a child, born without a father, should be sacrificed and its blood sprinkled over the site to cleanse it. Pliny records that the slaying of a human being was a highly religious act among the Britons, and the eating of flesh regarded as a "wholesome remedy." The Roman historian Diodorus Siculus states that the Irish ate their enemies, and the Greek historian and traveler Pausaniaus tells how the Galatian Celts ate the flesh and drank the blood of children. Solinus described the Irish tradition of washing the face in the blood of the slain, and imbibing it. The blood of dead relatives was also drunk by the Irish and this custom persisted into the sixteenth century.[14]

A favorite victim was a man between the ages of twenty-five and thirty who was "without spot and blemish."[15] As usual, Satan tries to counterfeit our Lord and Saviour Jesus Christ.

In the light of such evidence, it would be difficult for L'Engle to flatly deny the existence of such atrocities and maintain any credibility with knowledgeable readers. But she spends her whole book trying to justify the murders. She writes, "There is a theory that it was believed the Earth Mother demanded blood and that each year, perhaps at Samhain, there was human sacrifice. [And she admits this while calling Samhain a "holy time"!] If possible it was a prisoner. If not, then someone, usually the weakest in the tribe, would be laid on the alter and blood given to the ground."[16]

This is not true, but even if it were, is she attempting to make the atrocity more bearable? Is someone's life of less value because he is physically or mentally imperfect? This is exactly the same rationale Hitler used when he emptied all of the hospitals, nursing homes, and mental wards!

The story gets worse. Polly, who is posing as a goddess, is captured by an opposing tribe. The priest, who is a psychic healer, shows her the altar where he is going to kill her if the rains don't come. And what is her response?

> She thought of the healer holding his hands over Zachary with the delicacy of a butterfly, of her own experience of the healer holding his hands over hers, as warmth flowed through them. There had been incredible power and beauty in the old man's hands. Could he be a healer and yet with his healing hands take her blood to enhance his power? Could benign power and malign power work together? Mana power and taboo power were each an aspect of power itself. . . . But there was [a ley line] between Polly and the healer. Surely the loving power of Christ had been in those delicate hands. . . .[17]

Utter blasphemy! Christ's power does not reside in the hands of a butcher. L'Engle continually speaks of *mana* power, the power that creates, and *taboo* power, the power that destroys.[18] This is simply another form of the *Yin* and the *Yang*—the pagan belief that all power, good and evil, comes from the same source (as expressed in dualism). That God has two sides, light and dark. She complains that "we rational and civilized people have turned our back on the *dark side of God* because we are afraid of the numinous and the unexplainable"[19] (emphasis added).

Does God have a "dark side?" Absolutely not. So just what is this taboo power, this darkness that L'Engle urges her readers to embrace? According to Scripture, it is Satan. Throughout the Bible, darkness is used to describe Satan, the lost state of mankind, and the "outer darkness" of eternal damnation—not God. I John 1:5b tells us that "God is light and *in Him is no darkness at all*" (emphasis added). Once again, her theology is in direct conflict with the teachings of God.

In *An Acceptable Time*, Madeleine compares those who believe in the substitutionary atonement of Christ to murderous savages who slaughter human beings to satisfy Mother Earth.[20] And if this isn't enough, she goes on to quote the Roman Catholic Saint Columba as saying that Jesus Christ was his Druid. She then asserts that "Christ didn't just appear as Jesus of Nazareth two thousand years ago."[21] Just what is L'Engle saying? In *The Irrational Season*, L'Engle called Jesus "the man who housed" the Christ.[22]

While quoting St. Columba's assertion that Jesus was a Druid, she neglected to tell the readers that this same Catholic saint performed human sacrifice. According to the archaeologist Dr. Anne Ross, there is evidence that St. Columba sacrificed Oran (or Odran), one of his monks, to consecrate the foundations of his monastery in Iona.[23] It is difficult to believe that Madeleine L'Engle could be unaware of this fact since the story is also recorded in *Celtic Christianity*, an anthology published by Lindisfarne Press, which bears L'Engle's endorsement on the back cover.

Gods of the Druids

"This goddess," Polly mused, "and the Mother. Are they one and the same?"

Anaral punched down the risen dough. "To me, and to Karralys, yes. To those who are not Druids—Tav for instance—the goddess is the moon, and the Mother is the earth. For some, it is easier to think of separate gods and goddesses in the wind, in the oaks, in the water. But for me, it is all One Presence, with many aspects, even as you and I have many aspects." [24]

Dialogues such as these and the "bishop's" continual endorsement of this pagan goddess worship might leave a reader believing that the Druids worshipped the one true God. But that impression is false.

In actuality, the Druids were pantheists who worshipped a myriad of bloodthirsty deities. These were ruled over by an evil triumvirate, all of whom required human sacrifice, each preferring a different method of execution. Taranis, god of thunder, required prisoners of war to be burned alive in large wicker cages shaped as men. However, in some circumstances, three thunderous blows with an ax would suffice. Esus, the lord and master, preferred his victims to be hung or stabbed or both. Teutates, the overall god of the people, expected his offerings to be drowned in sacred pools and wells.[25]

Lindow Man was a three-fold sacrifice meant to implore the aid of all three gods. He had been dealt three blows with an ax while he knelt before his executioners. Then his unconscious body had been propped up and a garrote was secured around his neck—the equivalent of hanging. As he was being strangled, his blood was drained from his still living body from a surgical cut made in the jugular. Finally, the corpse was thrown into a four-foot-deep pool to simulate drowning.[26]

Doctrines of Demons

The Celts celebrated eight religious holidays, all of which were accompanied by sacrifice. (These are identical to the eight sabbats observed by witches and Satanists today.) Four holidays highlighted the farming year representing plowing, sowing, growing, and harvest.[27] The four major feasts were: Imbolc, 1 February, the feast of renewal dedicated to the goddess (and later Christian saint) Brigit; Beltain, 1 May, honoring the ancient god Belenos; Lughnaza, 1 August, the festival of the god Lugos; and Samhain, 1 November, the Celtic new year and feast of the dead, which was celebrated on 31 October.[28]

Beltain and Samhain were times of great fear and uncertainty. Huge bonfires were lit on these nights, and hundreds of people were burned alive to placate the ever-angry gods. "Beltain" literally means "Baal's fire," and most historians agree that this was a carry-over of the Baal worship in Canaan. On this night, cattle would be driven between the fires to ensure their fertility, accompanied by the agonizing screams of those dying in the flames (hence bone-fires, now contracted to bonfires). If this is similar to what the Canaanites practiced, it is no wonder that God ordered their extinction.

Samhain "was a night of divination and magic, where

the correct ritual must be performed in order to pacify
the super-natural forces which were believed to be everywhere in the world of men at that time."²⁹ Once again the
"bone-fires" would be lit, and many would die. And how
does L'Engle portray this unholy time? *She* calls it "holy."
In her story, Polly goes through the pool to meet the
Druids. She willingly puts on a silver crown with a crescent moon, the universal symbol of witchcraft, and joins
the circle where the fire is being passed. The Druids
dance around the fire, singing praises to their pagan
gods. "Polly's heart soared with the voices of the people
in and around the circle, so that she forgot her fear.
Slowly the song died away into a gentle silence."³⁰

How can a Christian's heart be uplifted by idolatry?
God demanded that we should have no other god before
Him. And whenever he sent his people to clean out this
detestable idolatry, He required that every grove and
temple be destroyed. God knew that if they were left
standing, people would soon go whoring after the old
gods. And that is exactly what has happened to the
temple sites of the Druids. Stonehenge is an excellent
example. Many believe that this was a place of Satan
worship and horrible human carnage. Yet thousands of
occultists, New Agers, and Druids flock there every year
to chant mantras, perform rituals, and experience altered states of consciousness. And what does L'Engle
think of Stonehenge? She claims it is holier than Christian churches. "The motive was certainly religious—behind the building of Stonehenge, that is—more truly
religious than the crude rituals and 'worship services'
that pass for religion in most of our churches today."³¹

The doctrines of the Druids are incredibly similar to
those of the New Age. But perhaps that should not be
surprising, since they all come from the same evil spiritual source. One of the most popular is reincarnation. A
belief in reincarnation is especially convenient in a religious society that demands large numbers of people to
feed its fires. The murders seem less horrid if everyone
believes that the dead will quickly live again. Also, this

doctrine deceives people into thinking that they will never face God in judgment.

Despite God's statement that "it is appointed unto man *once* to die," (Heb. 9:27) Madeleine L'Engle says that Christianity and reincarnation are compatible. In fact, she proposes her own particular brand of reincarnation in some of her books. (For a more complete discussion of this issue, see chapter 9.)

Druids "called themselves 'Creators of the Universe,' a title that indicates their high self-esteem. They clearly saw themselves as god incarnate."[32] New Agers echo this prideful boast. They teach that we are all God and as such are co-creators of the universe. Madeleine has even devoted an entire book, *And It Was Good: A Book of Beginnings* (published by the Christian press Harold Shaw Publishers), to this heresy. She further states that angels and God are one and the same, yet when Lucifer made this claim, he was cast from heaven and sentenced to eternal damnation. When Adam and Eve ate of the forbidden fruit in an attempt to gain godhood, they were cast from Eden, sealing the sinful state of all mankind.

This is what the Lord, our Redeemer, says to would-be creators: "I am the Lord who has made all things, who *alone* stretched out the heavens, who spread out the earth *by myself*, who foiled the signs to false prophets and makes fools of diviners, who overthrows the learning of the wise and turns it into nonsense . . ." (Isa. 44:24b-25, emphasis added).

As in most pagan cultures, the Celts had great regard for snakes. Nathair was their serpent god, and one of their goddesses was pictured with two snakes twined about her body, their heads resting upon her breasts. Druids kept live snakes for religious purposes and carried a *caduceus*, the staff of Mercury, depicting two serpents embracing one another.[33] Though Christians generally associate snakes with the Great Serpent, Satan, L'Engle shares the pagans deep reverence for these creatures. Throughout many of her books, she portrays them as wise, mystical teachers, discerners of men's character, and powerful protectors of the innocent. In *Many Waters*, she has a "seriphim," which shape-shifts into a snake, and in *An Acceptable Time*, the Episcopal priest summons a snake for assistance.

Druids also incorporated divination, witchcraft, astrology, the reading of omens, etc., into their "worship"— all practices that are condemned by God and forbidden to His people. L'Engle, however, promotes these items as God's gifts and sadly complains that "we've lost many gifts that were once available."[34] But there was nothing godly in the manner in which these "gifts" were employed. Druids would divine the future by stabbing a man in the midriff and observing the convulsions of his body and the pouring of his blood as he lay dying.[35] Others would foretell the future by watching the death throes of the human sacrifices upon the fires or by examining the entrails of humans and animals. This is a mighty poor substitute for the gifts of the Spirit described in the Bible.

God warns that in the last days men would no longer tolerate sound doctrine but would pursue false teachings that satisfy their sinful natures. Perhaps that is why Madeleine L'Engle and others have succeeded in introducing these heresies into the Church.

Druids: Past and Present

It is hard to pinpoint a date of origin for the Druids, but they appear to have been strongly entrenched in Great Britain by the third or fourth century B.C. When Roman Catholicism entered this area, it adopted many of the druidic customs, superstitions, symbols, holidays, and deities, making a "conversion" to Christianity easy. All but one of the eight holidays were "Christianized." The namesake goddess Brighit, known as St. Brigit, was said to be the reincarnation of the Virgin Mary, and a convent was dedicated in her honor.[36] St. Brigit was actually the daughter of a Druid priest, and the legends that surround her are filled with Druid-like spells and powers. At her monastery in Kildare, nuns kept a perpetual fire burning—at the same spot where druidesses had kept a similar fire burning to the goddess Brigit.[37]

There is evidence that many of the early Roman Catholic priests and monks embraced druidic, occult practices. A manuscript was discovered in the monastery of St. Gall dating from the eighth or ninth century containing magic spells for preserving butter and healing certain diseases.[38] As noted earlier, St. Columba is thought to have consecrated his monastery on Iona in the druidic fashion by sacrificing one of his monks.

Symbols of snake worship also filtered into the Roman church, adorning the crosses and crypts. The cross of Killamery, Kilkenny County, has two Irish serpents mounted on it, and several stones at Cashel Cathedral display sculptured snakes. "The Crozier, or Pastoral Staff of Cashel, which was found, bears a serpent springing out of a sheath or vagina."[39] Snakes mounted upon poles were also carried in Easter parades.[40]

Druid traditions were also preserved within Freemasonry, which is thought to have evolved from the Druids, or at least alongside of them. This connection is addressed in Gould's *History of Freemasonry.*[41] The three part structure of the masons is identical to the three offices of druidic priesthood: Ovates, Bards, and Druids. Also, "the secret teachings embodied therein are practically the same as the mysteries concealed under the allegories of Blue Lodge Masonry."[42]

Political and religious suppression forced the Druids to go underground. Many thought that the religion had disappeared, but it survived, handed down within families and villages, to resurface again in the early eighteenth century.

There are presently three main druidic colleges. The oldest was founded in 1717 by representatives from Britain, Scotland, and Ireland and is known as the Druid Order. The second one, the Ancient Order of Druids, was founded by Henry Hurles in 1781 and is a compromise between druidism and freemasonry. This branch of druidism has been particularly popular in Germany, Scandinavia, Australia, and the United States.

The third one was founded in Wales by a Welshman named Iolo Moganwg in 1792 and is known as the Gorsedds of Wales.[43] In fact, druidism has become so accepted socially that Queen Elizabeth II and the Prince of Wales both accepted posts as honorary Druids in the Wales Gorsedd.[44]

Madeleine L'Engle has her wish—there are Druids today. By 1988, there were estimated to be over one million adepts (spiritual masters), and the movement is growing. Her book, *An Acceptable Time*, is just the recruiting manual the movement needs to reach our young people. This book is on the suggested reading lists of many schools, both public and parochial. It paints a very attractive picture of the evil, ancient order of druidism, making L'Engle's trusting young reader easy prey for Satan's snare. Parents need to be aware of the battle that is raging for the minds and souls of our young people. Madeleine L'Engle has helped bring the battlefront into the church.

CHAPTER FOUR

OOOOOOOOOOOOOOOOOOOOOOOOOOOOOOOOOOOOOOOOOOOO

The Cathedral of St. John the Divine

"Perhaps we will once again be One when all the hungry sheep have broken down and leapt over the denominational barriers in order to be nourished together, and ultimately the Hierarchies will recognize that unity is already here, and can throw away all those millions of miles of red tape."

—Madeleine L'Engle, *The Irrational Season*, p. 142

A Personal Story

Madeleine L'Engle's story can be found in four of her books: *Circle of Quiet*, *The Summer of the Great-Grandmother*, *The Irrational Season*, and *The Two Part Invention*. It is in these books that we find proof of her close connection to the Cathedral of St. John the Divine and others in the New Age movement who have greatly influenced her writings and beliefs.

According to those sources, L'Engle became acquainted with the Cathedral of St. John the Divine through a series of circumstances.

Agnostics at Crosswicks

L'Engle's husband left the theater for a time, and they moved to Crosswicks, Connecticut. There, they ran a store. Before returning to New York, Madeleine and Hugh attended an Episcopal Church at Crosswicks, not because they believed in God, but because of their children.

. . . we discovered that we did not want our children to grow up in a world which was centered on man to the exclusions of god . . . I found myself earnestly explaining to the young minister that I did not believe in god, but I've discovered that I can't live as though I didn't believe in him. As long as I don't need to say any more than I try to live as though I believe in god, I would very much like to come to church—if you'll let me. So, I became the choir director.[1]

So, as an agnostic, L'Engle was allowed to direct the choir. One reason she accepted the position was because she didn't like the music and set about changing it. "The standard of music was low, what I called 'Blood of the lamb-y.'"[2]

During the entire time they lived at Crosswicks, neither Madeleine nor Hugh believed in God. She wrote with hostility, "It seems to me that we have been in the post-Christian world since 1054 when the Eastern and Western world split, or maybe even earlier when Constantine made Christianity mandatory instead of dangerous and forbidden."[3]

Madeleine Meets Tallis

When the children were still small, L'Engle's family left Crosswicks and moved back to New York, and Hugh returned to the theater. They placed the children in private schools, where Madeleine was asked to become involved in the general volunteer work of the school. She insisted on doing something at which she felt she was good, and because of her background in the theater, offered to direct the Episcopal school's Christmas program.

The play, as it turned out, was performed at the Cathedral of St. John the Divine. And it was there that she met Canon Tallis, an Episcopal bishop who later became a character in her books. They squabbled over her lack of concern with the chronology of the Christmas story, but she got her own way, convincing Tallis that the sequence didn't really matter as long as the point got across.

Tallis and L'Engle began building a lifelong friendship, and it was through Tallis that she got pulled into the Cathedral, although she was still a skeptic concerning Christianity. Because it was becoming increasingly more difficult for L'Engle to write at home, Tallis arranged for L'Engle to write in the Cathedral's library in the afternoons while Hugh took care of the children. Eventually, she was given her own office.

Madeleine at St. John the Divine

Today, Madeleine L'Engle continues to write most of her fantasy, poetry, and non-fiction books from her office at St. John, where she is also a volunteer librarian. It was there, probably in the largest New Age church in the world (as will be evidenced later in this chapter), where she earned the title "author-in-residence." Besides keeping an eight-room high-rise apartment in New York City, she also commutes from her Connecticut home to "serve her Work" during the week, with the helpful guidance of a Buddha statue sitting on her desk. "My white china Buddha can conceal as well as reveal truth," she claims.[4]

L'Engle, a long-standing member of the Cathedral's congregation, is not only a lay minister (sometimes giving sermons, lectures, workshops, and Lenten meditation) but is also on their ordination board. She is one of the final examiners of those about to be frocked. Because of her deep ties to the Cathedral itself, she uses it as the setting for many of the stories in her books, some of which we found to be morbid and depressing, but written as usual from her great imagination.

For example, buried within her book, *A Severed Wasp* (one of the Cathedral novels), are a bishop's confessions of his former homosexual lifestyle, detailing everything from gay bars to masturbation. He gives credit to a chaplain, who gave him whiskey and got him drunk, for his conversion to Christianity.[5] The bishop describes in detail grotesque war stories of removing a corpse's head by pulling off a helmet, and of cutting off someone's skin, mistaking it for a jacket.[6]

Serving the Work

L'Engle is one of the seven "artists-in-residence" at the Cathedral, whose leaders cling to the belief that "art is sacred" and magical—that the artist is simply an empty vessel through which the gift is given by the Masters of the Hierarchy (spiritual governing body of the solar system). The artists "serve the art," the sacred gift for humanity.

L'Engle believes that what she writes becomes reality, truth empowered, and takes on a life of its own. She also considers the characters of her books to be real, sometimes appearing out of nowhere. She speaks of them as living people, whose lives she follows and writes about from book to book. Hugh Franklin apparently expressed some concern about her tendency to confuse reality with fantasy. In one of her public appearances, she admitted, "My husband used to say that I never really knew, when I finished a book, what in it had really happened and what I had made up. The Austin family does a lot of things my family does, and uh, yeah, I do think I get them mixed up."[7]

Going Where It Leads

That aside, she says, "When it is time to start work, I look at everything in the pot, sort, arrange, think about character and story line. Most of this part of the work is done consciously, but then there comes a moment of unself-consciousness, of letting go and *serving the work*."[8] "The artist cannot change the work at whim, but can only listen, look, wait, and set down what is revealed."[9] "To *serve a work of art* is almost identical with adoring the Master of the Universe in *contemplative prayer*."[10] "It is a joy to be allowed to be the *servant of the work*. And it is a humbling and exciting thing to know that *my work knows more than I do.* . . . As I tried to serve it, I began to comprehend something about *listening to the work*, about going where it shoved me"[11] (emphasis added).

In *Arm of the Starfish*, Madeleine was surprised to see one of the book's characters suddenly appear as she was writing the novel. "There had been no Joshua in my plot, at all. I had a choice at that moment. I could ignore Joshua, refuse to allow him into my story. Or I could have faith in the creative process and listen to Joshua. . . . It has been pointed out to me that Joshua is a *Christ figure*. . . ."[12] As a faithful "servant of the work," she rewrote over one hundred pages of the book to fit him in. "Joshua" is the Old Testament form of the name "Jesus," she admits, and when this character suddenly appeared, complete with that name, she knew that, like Jesus Christ, he would have to die for a good cause. This "Christ figure" is described in the novel as a self-proclaimed heretic and agnostic.

Association Questioned

L'Engle's long-time association with St. John seems to be a touchy subject, especially when she's confronted about her involvement with the Cathedral. A Wheaton College official approached her with concerns from a Christian who had attended her lectures and questioned her affiliation with the New Age church. She responded by saying that she attends an Episcopal church in New York City known to be an evangelical parish, which is also attended by some Wheaton College graduates, that her office at St. John is in a building separate from the Cathedral where she serves as the volunteer librarian, a concession for having an office located in the library.

She indicated that many of the things said about the Cathedral of St. John the Divine were "unfortunately, true," but denied having any official connection with the Cathedral itself. All this she assured her concerned critic, despite her duties on the ordination board, many recorded lectures, video-taped sermons (wearing a ministerial robe), and publications advertising her upcoming appearances. Even her own itinerary, sent to the authors of this book by L'Engle's secretary, announces her "Lenten Meditations with Dean Morton at Cathedral of St. John the Divine," 28 February–11 April 1990 (Wednesdays in Lent), and teachings on "The Four Paths of Meister Eckhart," 3 March 1990.

Pantheism at St. John

It is at L'Engle's church of worship that the doors of
St. John's opened one Sunday and in waltzed Mignon the
elephant, wearing a flower necklace. Behind her, in de-
creasing sizes, were a "camel, a horse, a burro, a llama,
a goat, a monkey, a goose, a turkey, a parrot, a python
and assorted smaller animals."[13] Their handlers wore
Franciscan robes, armed with brooms and buckets, and
herded them down the aisle to be blessed.

From the pulpit, the dean of the Cathedral, James
Parks Morton, said that animals were there "to celebrate
Creation,"[14] and the *inter-relatedness* of all things. Morton
quoted Ghandi regarding the sins of irresponsible earthkeeping, while six thousand animal lovers and their pets
gathered before him. The 6 October 1991 gala event was
held in celebration of the Feast of St. Francis. "God bless
the universe and all the creatures in it, great and small,"
proclaimed Morton.

This was all happening, no less, to the musical back-
drop of Paul Winter's Consort performing the *Earth Mass*,
which included the cries of whales and wolves. All the
while, the Omega Liturgical Dance Company (also known
as the Forces of Nature Dance Company) went leaping
up and down the aisles at this bizarre cathedral circus.
The Forces of Nature rehearse six nights a week in their
studio in the Cathedral's crypt.[15] Paul Winter's orchestra
is well-known for performing the Winter Solstice Celebration (for the past thirteen years) to crowds as large
as twelve thousand people.

Needless to say, not everyone enjoyed the animal
service. There were those who felt it was a desecration of
something supposed to be sacred. Some were appalled.
The majority, however, ruled that "zaniness is next to
godliness."

A fellow researcher supplied the authors with an
article, from which the following was excerpted, providing an additional glimpse of the strange goings-on in the
sanctuary: "Just before the high altar at St. John's is a
real-live, gurgling swamp, complete with the native

plants, fish, crustaceans, and uncounted micro-organisms that give these ecosystems their remarkable life-nurturing abilities."[16] This little feature, that lets one sit with a clear view of the altar and watch the fish, was constructed by the Gaia Institute, also based in the Cathedral.

Big John

"Big John," the largest Gothic cathedral in the world, sitting on a thirteen-acre property, took a hundred years to build and is in an on-going construction mode to continue nearly for the next century. It embraces the idea of "an open mind" and of a pantheistic one-world religion. Dean James Parks Morton, who calls himself "The Very Reverend," claims that the jungle event was an attempt to revive the medieval cathedral tradition. His plans include having St. John set up to be the "sanctuary of the City," to serve as a "city center," in medieval fashion, drawing New Yorkers to its "festive celebrations." Morton, a Harvard graduate, doesn't want his cathedral to be a place where people become "overly concerned with what is officially religious and what is not . . ."[17] Obviously.

Shinto and Native American shrines are set up inside. Above the bays of stained glass windows are the austere offices of the "ecumenical" Temple of Understanding. The Gaia Institute, founded by James Lovelock, is also housed there, as is the Lindisfarne Association (an offshoot of Findhorn, a New Age community in Northern Scotland known for its gardens and nature spirits). The board of directors and Supporting Members list read like a "Who's Who" of international occultism.

Morton's idea was to build a house of prayer for all nations, all religions, with seven different chapels surrounding the main altar—an open place where ecumenical practice would include Franciscan relationships, a kind of mystical communion among all living things, even plants and animals. His masses include the prayers of Buddhists, Hindus, Moslems and Tai Chi rituals.

St. John's cornerstone was laid on 27 December 1892

with Episcopal officials believing that the greatness of
New York would depend on this cathedral. Work halted
occasionally due to wars and lack of money. One of its
chief fundraisers for a time was a "young lawyer named
Franklin Delano Roosevelt."[18] Morton was appointed dean
in 1972 to oversee an empty church and unfinished building that was, nonetheless, the largest Gothic cathedral
on the continent. His vision included more than anyone
knew. It would be a center for the one world religion.

Gargoyles and Spires

Dean Morton believes that completing the "house of
worship" for the city should be done in the thirteenth-
century Gothic tradition. He founded the Stoneyard Institute nearly ten years earlier and set up cutting and
carving sheds. Cranes were installed to lift and trans-
port the blocks of Indiana limestone throughout the process of building St. Peter's and St. Paul's towers, the
323-foot spires. English master masons, trained in medieval stone cutting, arrived to impart their craft to a new
generation of cathedral builders.

They recruited and hired sixty-five sixteen-year-old
young men and women of multiple nationalities from the
surrounding inner city for schooling as stone cutters,
using medieval instruments and fashioning stone after a
fifteen hundred-year-old Mayan tradition—part of a "sacred whole," as St. John's flier boasts. Grotesque-looking
gargoyles are chiseled from stone and set in place on the
Cathedral, jeering down and sticking tongues out at the
onlookers. Funding for the two-century-long project has
been supplied through gifts, including some quite large—
like the one for over a million dollars from international
financier and philanthropist J. P. Morgan.[19]

Underground Crypt

Beneath the Cathedral lies the world's largest underground Gothic crypt, a seldom-mentioned amenity of the
building. Not far from graves of some of the church's

hierarchy, one can sometimes find artists at work on the natural stage of what might appear to be the biggest sandbox in the world. Besides the rigorous nightly rehearsal of the Forces of Nature Dance Company, the crypt has been used for an experimental theater/opera production based on the first two parts of "The Oresteia" trilogy written twenty-four centuries ago by the Greek dramatist Aeschylus.

Where better to stage a pagan play than in a church crypt? *Furies* has been called "decidedly pagan in religious and philosophical outlook" and was performed only a few yards from the tombs of three Episcopal bishops. Only 150 persons can crowd into the crypt audience to experience "sacred and mysterious qualities of the space."[20] Some reported that they felt they were in "another world."

The idea for using the huge crypt evolved after the death of John-Michael Tebelak, the Cathedral's dramatist-in-residence (and author of the Broadway rock musical *Godspell*). Today, the cavernous crypt houses sculptors, textile-design apprentices, researchers, liturgical dancers, and craftsmen, and it provides some offices for others. One of the original Earth Day founders, John McConnell, had offices there for three years. There are those who believe that beneath the Cathedral lies a complex system of tunnels.[21]

Christa

In 1984, St. John's was in the headlines when Morton allowed the blasphemous "Christa," a female crucifix, to be displayed. "The Maundy Thursday services drew a gasp from the congregation when the Christus was, in fact, a Christa, complete with undraped breasts and rounded hips."[22] The work was created in 1975 by sculptor Edwina Sandys, forty-five-year-old granddaughter of Winston Churchill, for the United Nations' Decade for Women. To New York Suffragan Bishop Walter Dennis, it was another "desecration" of Christian symbols. How-

ever, Morton thought it sent a positive message to women.
Some believed it represented a "mystic Christian view
that sees Christ as our mother."[23]

St. John's pulpit guests have included the likes of
David Spangler, Earth Summit Secretary General
Maurice Strong, Jesse Jackson, Desmond Tutu, Robert
Kennedy, Madeleine L'Engle, Thomas Berry, Norman
Vincent Peale (33rd degree mason*), Margaret Mead,
Robert Redford, Rod McKuen, Kurt Waldheim, Jean
Houston, and the Dalai Lama, among others.

Morton has also shared services with Native American and Shinto leaders, according to Cathedral literature. In an interview, he said,

> At Pentecost we invited the head *rabbi* of New
> York, the Abbot of the *Zen* Community, Satchidi-
> nand—*Hindu* [the swami who blessed Ted Turner,
> Barbara Marx Hubbard, and Robert Muller at the
> Soviet-American Citizens Summit], Oren Lyons—
> an *American Indian*, the *head Imam at the mosque*
> and we all stood around the altar and prayed for
> peace in our own languages. Then we all received
> communion. Some church people said, "How can
> you do that? They don't know what they're receiv-
> ing!" I say, "Well, I don't really know what I'm
> receiving either."[24]

Episcopals Buying In

The Cathedral of St. John the Divine is the center of
some of the most innovative programs in ecology being
explored by religious institutions throughout the U.S.
and the world. That is why it has been dubbed "The
Green Cathedral." Under the visionary leadership of Dean
Morton, it has jumped ahead of other churches and for
thirty years has been ridiculed by the Episcopalian hierarchy. Now it has taken a leadership position in exalting

---

*In the article, "What Freemasonry Means to Me," by Dr. Norman
Vincent Peale, a 33rd degree mason, Dr. Peale states, "My grandfather was a Mason for 50 years, my father for 50 years, and I have
been a Mason for 60 years."[25]

the earth as a living, breathing organism (the Gaia theory) and in attempting to restore the "Goddess" to "Her" rightful place.

Madeleine L'Engle also supports this ecological theme:

> If we truly thought of the *earth as Mother* we could not do to her some of the things we have done . . . then *gender in rock* and *rose, tree* and *turnip, sea* and *seed, is a form of thanks and praise.*[26]

L'Engle also wrote an endorsement to *Something More*, a training manual for raising ecologically correct children, written by Jean Grasso Fitzpatrick. It contains easy-to-follow instructions for teaching your children how to reach "stillness"—altered states of consciousness—through Zen-like meditation so that they can "know God." Other projects include: teaching your child to be an "ecology detective," celebrating the United Nations Environmental Sabbath, and learning prayers, chants, and songs for worshipping the earth. Claiming "we are all spiritually connected with all creation," the author urges parents to "teach your children . . . that the earth is our mother. Whatever befalls the earth, befalls the children of the earth."[27]

In her endorsement, L'Engle says, "*Something More* is a book I want to give to all my friends who have young children. It is fresh and wise and definitely for the 1990s. It is brave enough to ask questions and then to refuse to give finite answers. Above all, it is a *loving* book."

Jean Fitzpatrick repays the gesture by recommending several of L'Engle's books in her glossary, along with the works of Matthew Fox, Thomas Berry, Carl Jung, Abraham Maslow, Elie Wiesel, Joseph Campbell, the Quaker Reader, Erick Fromm, and the music of Paul Winter Consort, including the Earth Mass/Missa Gaia.

The Bauhaus Movement

The sixty-two-year-old Morton is fulfilling a vision he's had since childhood: growing up amidst artists, actors, and musicians (his father was head of the Iowa University theatre department). His interest was piqued in high school by the exciting new movement called the "Bauhaus"—not just another style of design. Bauhaus set new standards for the underlying architecture of society and "propelled young Morton to Harvard to study under its shining light, German-born Walter Gropius," a political leftist who combined the "spiritual" with architecture and design. Bauhaus was the "New Architecture" of both design and societal development and taught that art, spirituality, and philosophy of a civilization must integrate and reflect the "forces" that made it possible. Thus, "the whole earth must become the Church"—"The Cathedral of Socialism."[28]

Morton prepared for the priesthood at Cambridge and set about to tackle the issues of poverty and urban decay in the cauldron of the inner city. In 1964, he "was called" to head the Urban Training Institute of Chicago; Sol Alinksy (*Rules for Radicals* author) was on the board, Andrew Young was on the faculty, and there Jesse Jackson founded operation PUSH. Morton became an "architect" priest and the Cathedral became a pantheon.*

New Age Cathedral

Shortly after he came to the Cathedral in 1972, Morton was introduced to New York author and Irish Druid William Irwin Thompson and his Lindisfarne Association.[29] Through these contacts, he met Rene Debos, a biologist and author of *Beast or Angel?*, *Choices That Make Us Human*, and *A God Within*, who, in Morton's words, "really turned me upside down." In the early 1970s, Morton began to learn new ways of describing the universe and man's relationship to it. He credits Thompson and Dubos with his "mind-altering experiences" that set the pace for the future. Morton identified his own

---

*In *Tarrytown*, during a November 1985 interview with Sally van Wagenen Keil, Morton talks about having the Hindu goddess Kali in his church. "Simplistic Westerners ask, 'How can you have a devil in your pantheon? Or, how can you worship a goddess that eats babies?' I'm not very interested in a goddess who eats babies, but I am interested in what that's trying to say. Within such totalities, it's possible to see how opposites assist each other."

task in life: "to put flesh on that planetary conceptualization."[30]

Four years prior, a few early environmentalists, including John McConnel, Margaret Mead, and Jose Arguellas, initiated the original Earth Day in 1968 on the spring equinox with a full-moon celebration. The Earth Day International organization was officed in the basement of St. John for three years. Earth Day impacted Morton's thinking, as did Amory Lovins (Rocky Mountain Institute), Thomas Berry (pantheistic Catholic theologian), Dubos, and others. Concerned about the fate of Mother Earth, Morton invited them to speak at the Cathedral.

Morton's views evolved "The Earth is God's Body, Jesus in Earth—God incarnate in the flesh of the earth, the flesh of the water, the flesh of the elements of creation and how that creation is suffering—the *passion of the creation*." A major sermon series was organized, called "The Earth's Sacred Voyage," blending spirituality and social action, turning St. John into a combination environmental think-tank, a switchboard for world religions, and a major center for the lively arts.[31]

James Lovelock (founder of the Gaia Institute, located at St. John's) gave his first public exposition on the "Gaia Hypothesis—the Earth is Alive." The series ended with Morton supposedly referring to the "*whole creation* as the body of Christ." Paul Winter was commissioned to write the liturgical "Missa Gaia" or Earth Mass, and since 1983 it has been revived every year on St. Francis of Assissi Day. Morton came to be known as the "Green Dean."[32]

Cathedral Goes International

In 1979, St. John's had the first Sun Day Celebration (in honor of solar energy and the Sun god) with speakers Margaret Mead (anthropologist), Robert Redford (actor),*

---

*Robert Redford is one of the movers and shakers for the development of the Green Party in America.

Gus Speth (president of the Washington-based World
Resources Institute), and others. Thousands came. Celebrations became part of the life of the Cathedral . . .
liturgy was sung and danced and spoken, and fairs were
held on behalf of the environmental groups.

Also, in 1979, St. John's took its turn to host the
annual four-day meeting of all the cathedral deans of
North and South America, as well as half-a-dozen English deans. The speakers were eco-theologian Thomas
Berry, Rene Dubos, and John and Nancy Todd (of the
new-age New Alchemy Institute).

Out of these early meetings, the Cathedral was able
to establish a number of different programs, linking the
issue of poverty and social justice with the issues of the
environment and ecology, education, religion, day care,
homelessness, job training, environment—*ALL*, Morton
believed, are *PART OF THE WHOLE*, which is the
HEALTH OF THE PLANET. Under the umbrella "City
and Planet: A Program for the Environment," the Cathedral has helped to gather important scientists, politicians, and artists of all nations and faiths for international conferences in Oxford and Moscow. Morton's ultimate vision was to help establish a "Spiritual United
Nations" to govern the whole earth.

The Cathedral of St. John the Divine is not hurting
for funds for their various programs. It is huge, with a
congregation in the thousands and a budget in the millions. Its influence extends across the globe.

CHAPTER FIVE

00000000000000000000000000000000000000000000000

St. John's Is Not Divine

The Temple of Understanding

To carry the connections further, the Mother of all New Age organizations behind the *Global Forum* just happens to be the Temple of Understanding, which is closely tied to the United Nations and is housed at Madeleine L'Engle's church, the Cathedral of St. John the Divine. Not surprising, James Parks Morton is the president of the Temple of Understanding. The Temple's purpose in the scheme of the New World Order is to facilitate the one world religion, through promoting both the acceptance and the embrace of all religions, beliefs, and rituals.

The Temple of Understanding was founded in 1960 by Juliet Hollister, a wealthy American socialite who refers to herself as a "housewife," with plans to erect a $5-million edifice for itself in Washington, DC, according to a 1962 news article.[1] It was to have been the temple of all temples for World Citizens, a group seeking funds to build a "Spiritual U.N." The project had a lot of support. Endorsers included the likes of: Secretary of Defense Robert S. McNamara; Socialist leader Norman Thomas; Chester Bowles, special advisor to the president; Thomas Watson, president of IBM; Eleanor Roosevelt; the United Lodge of Theosophists; New York City; and others.

According to a brochure issued from the Temple of Understanding (then-headquartered in Greenwich, Connecticut), "a wing of this modern day tower of Babel will be accorded to each of the six international faiths: Hinduism, Judaism, Buddhism, Confucianism, Christianity and Islam."

Other endorsers at that time of the edifice were listed: Jack Benny; Douglas MacArthur II; Max Lerner of the *New York Post*; Fred Jordan, president of International Spiritualists; Philip Linnik, director of Universal Brotherhood Center; James A. Linen, president of Time-Life, Inc.; the president of Guatemala; and more.

A 1962 news article brought out this interesting piece of information: The symbolism planned for the building dated back to black magic practiced by the high priests of ancient Egypt. The building was to have contained "a giant eye" and "a circular pool of water which reflects light beamed onto it by a dome faceted to look like a many-colored diamond."[2]

Besant's Temple

Funds had been raised to build a similar shrine in London by the late occultist Mrs. Annie Besant (thirty-year international president of the Theosophical Society), working closely with Nehru and Krishna Menog. She was a founder of the Fabian Parliamentary League (whose membership included George Bernard Shaw). Besant's shrine contained a mural of a six-pointed Theosophical star made of two interlocking triangles connected by a serpent. "This theme is repeated in the Temple of Understanding," the article read.

Temple of Understanding Meditation Room

The plans for the Washington, DC, temple included a Meditation Room, resembling the United Nations Meditation Room in New York City, which has as its altar a huge chunk of polished ore, a sacred stone on which a beam of light plays. The late Dag Hammerskjold, the U.N. secretary general, described this stone as "an altar to universal religion. The altar is the symbol of the God of all."[3]

The Temple of Understanding's Meditation Room was to be known as the "Hall of Illumination," where "the Illuminati, Masters of Wisdom, Our Leaders of the Temple of Understanding [will] train the public in the new humanistic cult." Their intentions: to create a "new type of mystic . . . to be distinguished by his ability to see God immanent in all faiths and not just in his own brand of religious belief—the New World Religion."⁴ (This same article mentions that "the New Group of World Servers had been holding 'full moon meetings at the Carnegie Endowment International Center in New York on December 21, 1961.'")

Temple's Temple Didn't Fly

Plans somehow were changed, and the Temple of Understanding moved to New York, where it set up headquarters at the Cathedral of St. John the Divine. Executive director for the Temple, "The Rev." Daniel L. Anderson, explained, "Our office is here in NYC, and next month [will] open a chapter in India (New Delhi). We have decided not to pursue the Washington, DC, land/ location or building of a temple. Instead, we are initiating a diverse range of programs and persons and groups around the world to live and act together interdependently."⁵

World Interfaith Headquarters

According to the Temple of Understanding's own literature, it is the world's second oldest international interfaith organization, just behind the *World Congress of Faiths*, founded in England in 1935 by Sir Francis Younghusband. The Temple began through the efforts of a strange group of "Founding Friends," including world leaders Eleanor Roosevelt, Albert Schweitzer, Thomas Merton, the Dalai Lama, U Thant, Pope John XXIII, Pope Paul VI, ecumenical patriarch Athenagoras, Madalyn Garabaldi, Dr. Radhakrishnan (vice-president of India), Tenko Nishida, S. Zalman Shazar, Anwar el-Sadat, Jawaharlal Nehru, and Sir Zafrulla Khan, president of the International Board of Justice.

The "Friends" assisted the founder, Juliet Hollister (wife of J. Dickerman Hollister), in establishing a world interfaith center based in the U.S. Additional sponsors have included John D. Rockefeller II, Margaret Sanger (founder of Planned Parenthood), International Planned Parenthood, Defense Secretary Robert McNamara, Pearl Buck, Norman Thomas, Bishop James A. Pike, Brooke Harp (an assistant to former President Kennedy), Douglas McArthur II, the president of IBM, the Society of Friends [Quakers], the Jewish Theological Seminary, the Unitarian Fellowship, and Carlos Romulo of the Philippines.[6]

Temple Declaration

During the mid-1980s, *New Genesis*, a book that called for a new global spirituality, prompted Hollister and her friends to ask Robert Muller (then assistant secretary-general of the U.N.) to draft a "Declaration of the Unity of the World," which is quoted below. Muller's monistic theology is wrapped up in his statement, "We are living Earth. Each of us is a cell."[7]

This New Age draft led to the Temple of Understanding sponsoring a meeting on *Mount Sinai* in October of 1984 to thrash out inter-religious consensus on:

1. The *oneness of human family*, irrespective of color, sex, creed, nation—or any other distinctive characteristic.

2. The harmonious place of the individual person in the total order of things, as a *unique entity of divine origin*, with physical, mental, moral, and spiritual aspirations, and with basic relationship to the universe and eternity.

3. *The importance of religion, prayer, meditation spiritual exercises, contemplation, and the inner search as links between human life and the universe.*

4. The existence of an *incipient conscious and heart of humanity*, which speaks for what is good and against what is bad for humans; which advocates and fosters understanding, *cooperation,* and altruism instead of division, struggle, and indifference among nations.

5. The value of dedicated service to others, with a compassionate response to human suffering, with special attention to the poor, handicapped, the elderly, refugees, the rejected, and the lonely.

6. The *duty to give thanks* [to whom?] and express gratitude for the abundance of life which has been given to humanity, an abundance not to be selfishly possessed or accumulated, but to be shared and given generously to those who are in need, with *a sense of social justice.*

7. *The need for ecumenical agencies and world religious organizations to foster dialogue and collaborative arrangements, and to bring the resources and inspirations of the religions to bear upon the solution of world problems.*

8. A rejection of violence as being contrary to the sanctity and uniqueness of life, and an *affirmation of the law of love* and compassion as the great transcending force which alone can break the nemesis of war and violence.

9. An acceptance of the precept—"Thou shalt not kill, not even in the name of a nation or a faith."

10. *The evolutionary task of human life and society to move through the eternal stream of time towards interdependence, communion, and an ever-expanding realization of Divinity.*[8] (emphasis added)

Perhaps the Temple of Understanding group should have been making trips *around* Mt. Sinai. Could the reason for taking this document to the top of the mountain be that they were taking their ten new "Commandments" to a face-to-face encounter with their "god"?

Dr. Robert Muller, author of this declaration, happens to be a Fellow of the Center for World Thanksgiving Commission, a tax-exempt foundation that built Thanks-Giving Square in downtown Dallas in 1976. Thanks-Giving square is a U.N. sponsored meditation garden for World Religions depicting mankind's divine oneness. Touted as "an island of serenity" amid skyscrapers, the garden contains an elaborate white marble spiral chapel, which reminds one of a large fruit roll-up standing on end. There, the Dalai Lama, the archbishop of Canterbury, and John Templeton have spoken. President Bush made an appearance in 1991. Its declaration of *at-one-ment* is signed by Juliet Hollister (Temple of Understanding), the Buddhist Churches in America, Dr. Herbert W. Chilstrom (bishop of Evangelical Lutheran Churches in America), and Rabbi L. A. Hoffman (Hebrew Union College).

The concept of Thanks-Giving Square was suggested by Zen Buddhist contemplative Benedictine monk, Brother David Steindl-Rast, who teaches at Esalen and was a friend of Thomas Merton. Steindl-Rast is a member of Planetary Citizens, whose purpose is to serve as the vanguard for "the Reappearance of the Christ." He was also involved in the Cathedral of St. John the Divine, exploring meditation styles with Rabbi Herbert Weiner, author and scholar in the fields of Jewish mysticism and Hasidism.

Hollister Promotes New Age

Juliet Hollister was recently seen on a Public Broadcasting Network television program hyping the New Age movement. It went like this:

> Helping to usher in this Wisdom from the East was a housewife from Greenwich, Connecticut. She was having lunch with a friend and got an idea for a spiritual United Nations, an organization that would bring together the world's leaders. Henry Luce heard about this and put a feature article in *Life Magazine* about Judith Hollister's obsession.

Hollister responded:

> We began to grow and we've been continuing to grow, and then we began having conferences at Calcutta with Thomas Merton, and then at Geneva, and then at Harvard Divinity School. And the last was in England, of which we co-sponsored with an organization called the Global Forum, at Oxford University, which was a gathering of scientists and religious leaders and parliamentarians—to discuss the future of the planet and what we could

do about it—which included Carl Sagan and Tom
Berry and Dalai Lama, the archbishop of Canterbury.

It's very exciting for a woman my age, who watched
the beginnings of the New Age in 1940s, a little
trickling of beginnings. And to see it is expanding,
not just with the Temple of Understanding, but
with a million thousand different ways—of wonderful people, like Bernie Siegel, Jean Houston
and all of the people that we all know so well,
who've led to this new way of thinking. And it
continues to grow and grow. Grow and grow and it
just causes me to say how wonderful and beautiful
and Praise the Lord![9]

The TV documentary, called "Voices of the New Age,"
included interviews with Jean Houston, David Spangler,
Bernie Siegel, Peter Russell, and others. The Temple of
Understanding was acknowledged for giving support to
the production.

Slowly Going Global

However, it hasn't always been an easy road for the
Temple of Understanding. In the beginning, Hollister's
ideas for a spiritual U.N. weren't well-received until the
Connecticut "housewife" jetted around the world to en-
list the endorsement and help of an unusually mixed
bag—Islamic scholars, Hindu teachers, Buddhist think-
ers, Jewish leaders, and Protestant and Catholic theologians.

Eight years later, in 1968, Spiritual Summit I was
held in Calcutta, India. The star speaker was mystic
Thomas Merton, the Trappist monk and author who died
a few months later in Bangkok when he accidentally
touched a live electric wire. He delivered the closing
address, embracing strong pro-Communist and one-world
policies.

More conferences were held that included Buddhists,
bishops, deans, rabbis, graces, abbots, swamis, Sufies,
shamans, priests, patriarchs, Wiccans, gurus, vicars, and
assorted divines from a dozen major religions, represent-

ing 2.5 billion people. Whenever the spiritual jamborees
were held in New York, a number of the activities took
place at the United Nations.

Summit Conferences

The Temple of Understanding has fostered worldwide interfaith dialogue that has caught on fire. At its
heart is the ancient dream of accelerating the course of
the evolution of mankind to its final destiny—the Omega
Point—where individual souls cease to exist separately
but fade into the cosmos, an orderly harmonious whole—
the ultimate godhood.

The 1970 Spiritual Summit in Geneva brought to-
gether representatives from the World Council of
Churches, the World Congress of Faiths, the Russian
Orthodox Church, Serbian Church, the International
Court of Justice, Divine Knowledge Society, Princeton
Theological Seminary, Howard University, the Pathfinder
Fund, and more.

October 1971 saw the third Spiritual Summit confer-
ence at Harvard Divinity School and included Princeton
Theological Seminary, along with the Wainwright House.
The theme was "Religion in the Seventies."

The Fourth Spiritual Summit conference was held at
Cornell University at Ithaca, New York, in May of 1974.
The theme: "Toward World Community." Focusing on
education, representatives converged together from the
Association of World Colleges and Universities, Dag
Hammerskjold College, Friends World College, United
Nations University, Universities in the Quest for Peace,
Institute for World Order, and the World Conference of
Religion and Peace.

In October of 1975, a colorful and dramatic proces-
sion of about two hundred religious dignitaries from all
over the world, kicked off Spiritual Summit Conference
V at the Cathedral of St. John the Divine at the United
Nations and the Waldorf-Astoria Hotel. St. John's Dean
James Parks Morton, president of the Temple of Understanding, gave the welcoming address and Dr. Jean

Houston (a director of the Temple of Understanding) introduced the keynote speakers: Dr. Margaret Mead (who wore a black robe and carried her distinctive walking stick) and Kurt Waldheim, secretary general of the United Nations. Panel speakers included Dr. Robert Muller, Dr. Edgar Mitchell (former astronaut), Dom Leclercq (Roman Catholic theologian from Luxembourg and Rome), Rabbi Herbert Weiner, ambassadors, Hopi medicine men, Shinto priests, Zen Buddhists, Muslims, and a Unitarian minister. The program opened with a meditation given by guru Sri Chinmoy, director of the United Nations Meditation Group.

Jean Houston, conference chairman, read the Joint Statement of Spiritual Leaders:

> The delegates of the Conference, "One is the Human Spirit," propose that the time is ripe for the religions of the world to bring together in concert their several visions in aid of the United Nations in its endeavor to build a better human society. To this end, we strongly *recommend the United Nations consider the creation of an agency* which will bring the much needed resources and inspirations of the spiritual traditions to the solution of world problems.[10] (emphasis added)

In June of 1980, the directors of the Temple of Understanding voted unanimously to sponsor the formation of a World Monastic Council. Its purpose—to be an international network of monks, nuns, scholars, theologians, and laity from diverse religious traditions, both East and West, who would work together to create new forms of community for the global society of the future—to work for the awakening of spiritual consciousness (godhood).

Around 1982, during the time the Temple directors had their executive office at the Wainright House in Rye, New York, they attempted to purchase the pre-revolutionary Manor House, where George Washington held many planning sessions. It was adjacent to their own eighteen acres of forest land overlooking the Potomac in Washington, DC—where they planned to build their temple. The Manor House was to serve as the headquarters of the World Monastic Council, creating a "sacred space" in our national capital. Plans were aborted in favor of their current home in the Cathedral of St. John the Divine.[11]

Oxford Conference

The Temple of Understanding collaborated with the global Commission of Parliamentarian Leaders in early 1985 and gave birth to the Global Forum. The result was the beginning of worldwide conferences with an interfaith punch—a movement geared to "global responsibility"—unlike any other up to this time. Global Forum is the strongest vehicle the New Agers and occultists have to use to merge the political with the spiritual.

The Dalai Lama made the following observations to the delegates at the Oxford Conference: "Sometimes I call our planet our mother. Because of the planet, each human being existed. Now it seems our mother planet is telling us, 'My children, my dear children, behave in a more harmonious way. My children, please take some care about me.'"

April of 1988 saw the first international conference of the Global Forum, sponsored in part by the Temple of Understanding and co-chaired by James Parks Morton, president of the Temple. Called the Oxford Global Survival Conference, the emphasis was on the *prolific and renegade human species* that is *devouring the planet*. Addressing what was determined to be the "planetary crisis" of overpopulation were participants Carl Sagan; the Dalai Lama; James Lovelock; Rev. Luis Dolan; the archbishop of Canterbury; Paul Temple,* chairman of the board of the Institute of Noetic Sciences; Dr. Fred Sai, World Bank advisor on population issues; the leader

---

*Paul Temple and his wife Diane are executive committee members of the Temple of Understanding and played leading roles at the New Age Soviet-American Citizen Summit, held in Alexandria, Virginia, in February 1988. The Summit was developed by their friends Barbara Marx Hubbard, Rama Vernon, and Soviet Henrik Borobik. Temple saw himself as the "bridge" between Christians and New Agers and,

of the Green Belt movement; representatives of the Soviet Academy of Sciences; the MacArthur Foundation;
the Buddhist community; and assorted others.

Over two hundred leaders of the world's spiritual
traditions and members of parliaments on five conti-
nents concluded that they would identify themselves as
responsible *world citizens*, in an effort to *dismantle arms*
and promote "*cooperation*" among all peoples and sectors
of society; they would develop *new modes of education,
protect the planet*, and identify the "*appropriate balances
between resources and population*." Above all, they would
support the United Nations.[12]

Wichita

In October of 1988, the Temple of Understanding
made another leap toward the new world religion. As a
major contribution toward organizing the first North
American Interfaith Conference, the Temple of Understanding held "A North American Assisi," in Wichita,
Kansas. According to the press, 235 visitors gathered for
a multi-religious meeting, representing twelve of the
world's major religions, pursuing "universal understanding" and touting, "*We are all brothers!*"

Faith delegates represented Jains, American Indians, Christianity, Judaism, Buddhism, Hinduism, Islam,
Shintoism, Bahaism, Unitarian Universalism, Sikh, and
Zorastrianism. Some spanned more than one faith, such
as John L. Jory, a Quaker from California who is also a
practicing Buddhist. He hailed the conference as "the
direction of the future." The Wichita host was Rev. James
Bell, executive director of Wichita's Inter-Faith Ministries (and of the Washington, DC-based *Interfaith Impact Magazine*).

---

in fact, took credit for getting members of the Communist party and
one hundred New Agers invited to the Presidential National Prayer
Breakfast at the Pentagon, as well as the National Prayer Breakfast
for Israel during the same week. He was also a key player for the
"Bridging through Christ" conference held at Gold Lake Ranch in
Colorado (October 1987), co-hosted by Barbara Marx Hubbard and
Doug Coe.

The conference was named after a meeting held two years earlier, in Assisi, where Pope John Paul II was the host at a prayer-for-peace gathering of representatives of the same twelve faiths that met in Wichita.

Seattle

In the 1990s, the interfaith network, added more religious faiths to its roster. In a historic meeting in Seattle, in July 1990, nearly one hundred members of fifteen faiths (including Latter-Day Saints and Wiccan) and spiritual organizations in the U.S. and Canada joined in a three-day North American Interfaith Conference. It was the culmination of a five-year effort to adopt a constitution that would establish a national religious group—the North American Interfaith Network (NAIN).

"We've known through the ages that there is one religion, though it comes in many forms; and one God, who comes in many names," said NAIN's newly elected co-chairman and Presbyterian minister from Buffalo, Charles White.[13]

Plenary speaker Dr. Anantanand Rambachan, a Hindu scholar and professor at Olaf College in Minnesota, said, "In striving to create a just and peaceful world order, we must draw on the wisdom, critical insights and resources of all the world's religious traditions . . ."[14]

NAIN has published an interfaith directory listing over 125 interfaith organizations in the United States and Canada, available from the Temple of Understanding for $15.

Moscow—Ommming with Gorby

[During mid-January of 1990] an ecumenical group of spiritual leaders—ranging from several garbed rabbis, long-bearded Russian Orthodox priests, and robed Hindu swamis to brilliantly plumed Native American shamans—together with parliamentarians from around the world and a collection of environmentally concerned scientists met in Armand Hammer's conference center . . . for the

Global Forum on the environment and the Survival and Development of Humanity.[15]

Global Forum's first major conference included Soviet counterparts to the parliamentary, spiritually, and
environmentally correct leaders from around the world.
The gathering was officially co-hosted by the Supreme
Soviet, the Soviet Academy of Sciences, and the "Religious Communities of the Soviet Union." When President Gorbachev spoke, bishop James Parks Morton listened—from the speakers' platform. Gorbachev called
for environmental protection, including the need for the
"Zelenyi Krist," or Green Cross,* sort of an organized
band-aid for Mother Earth—this from a man whose leadership has caused much human and environmental devastation in many lands.

The application of the Green Cross is quite broad:
from promoting community service to providing volunteer helpers and watchdogs over the Third World countries. Cleaning up one's own backyard should teach the
young to be good little "earth stewards," say the leaders.
A call for drastic changes in everyone's lifestyle—for the
good of the whole—was made to *SAVE THE EARTH.*

The meeting started with an invocation by "a frail
Hindu swami draped in an ochre robe and daubed with
white body paint," who asked the audience to "repeat
after me, three times: *Ommm . . . ommm . . . ommm.*"
In no time, this Ghandi-like figure had Gorbachev and
the whole room "*omming* away in this citadel of failed
materialism while the portrait of Lenin, frozen in time,
glowered in the background."[16] Everything was disinte-
grating around them, and no wonder. In the Soviet Union,

---

*Not only did Gorbachev call for the International Green Cross, but
the NACCE (North American Conference on Christianity and Ecology) did, as well. In fact, this earth-oriented group is calling for
"environmental ethics education" for inner city youth and is working
in cooperation with the Earth Island Institute (named in the *New Age
Dictionary*) to apply the Green Cross to forest restoration, using
churches to recruit members for volunteer work. *Earthkeeping* author and director of Au Sable Institute for Environmental Studies,
Dr. Calvin DeWitt, former professor at Calvin College, is the chairman of the board of directors for NACCE.

New Age occultism was rapidly becoming the religion of choice for many of the Russian people.

The Moscow meeting helped to establish the Global Forum. Its co-chairman—none other than the president of the Temple of Understanding and the dean of the Cathedral of St. John the Divine—James Parks Morton.

Full Moon Gathering

San Francisco hosted another unusual convention, the Assembly of World's Religions, in August of 1990. This time, a new face appeared at the event, organized by the International Religious Foundation. The meeting was sponsored by none other than the Unification Church's founder, leader, and "messiah," Sun Myung Moon.

However, to the surprise of many, Moon made his claim to be the "Messiah" in front of one plenary gathering:

> The world needs to find the True Parent who can liberate it from Satan's love, life and lineage. This person is the Messiah. . . . Before this world can enter into the realm of true love and true family, the True Parents' position has first to be established. To help fulfill this very purpose I have been called upon by God. The mission of the Messiah is thus the cosmic mission which all religions are now undertaking.[17]

The inter-faith fashion show, as it turned out, involved participants wearing their traditional costumes or liturgical attire—and sharing faiths, dances, music, and poetry. Workshops included one that suggested that all Israeli children be taught Jewish *and* Muslim religious stories. The group had no Jewish or Muslim representatives, however. A Zorastrian fire ceremony was performed in a tent on the Hyatt Regency Hotel's roof; Native Americans and Buddhists meditated; and Latter-Day Saints, Africans, Jains, and Unificationists did their own form of worship. The conference spanned the Jewish Sabbath. The next assembly is to be held in 1993.

1893 - 1993

The Temple of Understanding plays hardball when it comes to the world religion for the New Age. In August of 1993, the Temple of Understanding and three other international inter-faith organizations will oversee the 100th anniversary worldwide celebration of the 1893 Chicago World Parliament of Religions at a gathering called "A Vision of Interfaith Co-operation in the Twenty-first Century." Besides the Temple of Understanding, co-sponsors of the multi-faith event are the International Association for Religious Freedom, World Congress of Faiths, and the World Conference on Religion and Peace.

The 1893 meeting provided a medium where many Americans were introduced to such Eastern religions as Hinduism, Islam, Buddhism, Jainism, Shintoism, Confucianism, Taoism, Zoroastrianism, and Bahai.

Ron Kidd of the Midwest Buddhist Council, administrator of the 1993 parliament, said the nineteenth-century event helped to launch the *comparative study of religion*** at the college and seminary levels. "We don't want or need to duplicate what's going on in education circles," he said. Instead, 1993 organizers hope to eventually push New Age religion into such areas as health, ecology, poverty policies, and economics, as well as personal spiritual growth.

According to a Christian News article, although the 1993 parliament has been endorsed by mainline bodies like the Roman Catholic Archdiocese of Chicago, the Evangelical Lutheran Church in America, and the Chicago branch of the Christian Church (Disciples of Christ), its major organizers have been representatives of the American Islamic College and the Vivekanadna Vedanta Society (Hindu), both of Chicago, along with the Bahais in Wilmette, Illinois.[18]

Unlike many Christian leaders today who are not willing to take a stand against apostasy, the late arch-

---

*One of the basic principles of the Theosophical Society is promoting the study of Comparative Religion. The Society is active in more than sixty countries and its world membership is well over 30,000.

bishop of Canterbury dared to stand up for righteousness. He declined an invitation to Chicago 1893, saying that Christianity was the only true religion and that participation in such a conference implied that the other religions were equal to Christianity.

An even stronger condemnation of the 1893 meeting came from E. J. Eitel, a missionary in Hong Kong, who accused the organizers of "unconsciously planning treason against Christ [by] playing fast and loose with . . . false religions."[19] The Bible warns about such a time as this, when a great falling away from the truth of the Word of God will occur, before the Antichrist is revealed (2 Thess. 2:3).

Children Targeted

The Temple of Understanding claims to offer something for everyone, including our children. It just so happens that school libraries throughout the United States can become recipients of award-winning films on Eastern religions that have been made available through the Hartley Film Foundation, in conjunction with the Temple of Understanding.

By promoting the concept of teaching "about" religion in schools, teachers are allowed to get away with indoctrinating captive audiences of children in the classrooms through "new" curricula and by showing religious videos by filmmakers like the Hartley Film Foundation on the TV sets already provided by Channel One.* The price is insignificant. Children can be proselytized for just the cost of duplicating and mailing the tapes.

The Hartley Film Foundation productions feature videos on New Agers, such as Huston Smith, Alan Watts, and Joseph Campbell. Titles currently being offered are:

---

*The controversial Channel One is an in-house TV news program that has been accepted in more than 9,300 public and private schools, reaching over six million children. Channel One lures subscribers by offering free TVs, VCRs and satellite dishes. Students are forced to watch twelve minutes of slanted Whittle Communications-managed news reports spiced with two minutes of commercials.

—*Buddhism: The Path to Enlightenment*
—*Hinduism and the Song of God*
—*Requiem for a Faith (Tibetan Buddhism)*
—*Taoism*
—*Trip to Awareness: A Jain Pilgrimage to India*[20]

It's interesting that the list does not include any film on Christianity.

The *Temple of Understanding Newsletter* states: "We are encouraged by the fact that teaching 'about' religion in the schools is receiving official approval in a growing number of states."[21] A recent article in *The Wall Street Journal* backs them up, they claim, pointing to a few states in the U.S. that have offered pilot programs with a religious-liberty curriculum issued by First Liberty Institute, a coalition of educators and religious groups formed in 1988 and headquartered in Fairfax, Virginia.

According to their own literature, Charles Haynes, a former religion professor and director of the Institute, has said that

> growing numbers of educators throughout the United States recognize that study *about* religion in social studies, literature, art and music is an essential part of a complete public school education. States and school districts are issuing new mandates and guidelines for the inclusion of teaching *about* religion in the curriculum. As a result, textbooks are expanding discussions of religion's role in history and culture, and many new supplementary materials concerning religion in history are being developed.[22]

Unfortunately, these curricula usually spend a great deal of time on pagan religions and barely give Christianity an honorable mention. Nor do they accurately present the major role Christianity played in the formation and early years of our nation.

First Liberty Institute

The brainchild of the privately funded Williamsburg Charter Foundation, the First Liberty Institute is an independent, non-profit organization also funded by private foundations (including the Carnegie Foundation) with the sole purpose of introducing educators led by former education commissioner Ernest L. Boyer. Boyer, President of the Carnegie Foundation for the Advancement of Teaching, announced the ambitious program to train teachers to "teach about religion," religious liberty, and civil values in the public schools.

The Carnegie Foundation, which has funded the Council on Foreign Relations (CFR) and other New World Order organizations, also calls for new steps to "ensure readiness" for all the nation's children by the year 2000. If this program is successful, the raising of our children will shift to the government. Boyer states, "What we propose is a decade-long campaign on behalf of the children, one in which *everyone* is involved and *no child is left out*."[23] Little Johnny could become a Buddhist world citizen laborer. (Ernest Boyer authored the 1983 report on public schools, "A Nation at Risk," which stimulated many of the radical changes taking place in public education.)

Williamsburg Charter

In a brief conversation, Dr. Oz Guinness, the former executive director of the now-defunct Williamsburg Charter, described the organization as "an ad hoc bicentennial celebrating the First Amendment." He went on: "Its most enduring product was the curriculum for the public schools. And that's been taken over by a new foundation, called the First Liberty Institute." Consequently, the lethal Williamsburg Charter curriculum has been integrated into the First Liberty Institute curriculum. Both curricula appeal enormously to New Agers and globalists, such as St. John's Temple of Understanding.

The First Liberty Institute, housed at George Mason University, has been training social studies teachers from around the country in the use of the New Age curriculum designed for elementary, junior-high, and senior-high student. Parents participate in an exercise where fifth-graders are asked to find out where their ancestors came from, whether their ancestors were part of a religious community, and whether religion played a role in their family's past—actually, no one's business, outside the family—but another way for teachers to build portfolios on students. The curriculum gets worse as it progresses through high school.

The lessons, called "Living With our Deepest Differences," are being adopted in school districts around the country through global education, or what Haynes calls "multi-cultural education." The curriculum was drafted with the help of the National School Boards Association, university education departments, and faith communities including the American Jewish Committee, the U.S. Catholic Conference, the National Council of Churches, and the National Association of Evangelicals. Oddly enough, it also has the support of Americans United for Separation of Church and State.

The Temple of Understanding has been involved with seminars and workshops given at numerous schools and colleges. Some of these are listed below:

Choate School, Wallingford, Connecticut
Concord Academy, Concord, Maine
Emma Willard School, Troy, New York
Kent School, Kent, Connecticut
Koinonia Foundation, Baltimore, Maryland
Sarah Lawrence College, Bronxville, New York
The Ethel Walker School, Simsbury, Connecticut
Wainwright House, Rye, New York

The Temple of Understanding describes itself as a non-profit educational corporation and non-governmental organization (NGO) *affiliated with the United Nations.*[24]

Lindisfarne

The Lindisfarne Association first began in Southampton, New York, as a New Age commune and was funded by Laurance S. Rockefeller and Sydney and Jean Lanier. The founder and director, William Irwin Thompson, studied at the esoteric human potential movement center, Esalen Institute, in Big Sur, California, and was inspired by founder Michael Murphy's ability to merge Eastern occult religion with Western psychology.[25]

Thompson, who had been raised in "orthodox Roman Catholicism," left his MIT teaching position and traveled the world, exploring the mystic roots of occult science and finding ways to bring Eastern meditation into philosophy, science, and art. He studied with David Spangler at Findhorn in northern Scotland and at Sri Aurobindo's Auroville in India, among other occult establishments.[26]

It was Thompson who had greatly influenced James Parks Morton of the Cathedral of St. John the Divine in the early 1970s. Encouraged by Morton and Nancy Wilson Ross (*World of Zen* author), Lindisfarne began a working relationship with both the Zen Center in San Francisco and the Cathedral in New York, making Lindisfarne both ecumenical and national.

Morton offered to house Lindisfarne's program at the Cathedral from the very beginning of its activities in 1973. Thompson instead leaned toward a contemplative and communal mode for his group and went to Southampton with Morton's blessings.

Maurice Strong and Colorado

In April of 1979, Thompson was attending the Solar Village Conference of the New Alchemy Institute where he bumped into Maurice Strong, under secretary-general of the United Nations. Strong, who had purchased a rather large ranch of 160,000 acres in the Baca, offered the Irish Druid nearly 80 acres if he would bring Lindisfarne to Colorado.[27]

A few weeks later in May, Thompson was four-wheeling near Crestone, Colorado, with John Todd (of New Alchemy), Mary Catherine Bateson (daughter of Margaret Mead and Gregory Bateson), and Maurice Strong when his "radar" went up and he pointed to "the spot" of Lindisfarne's future home.

The Grail

In August of that same year, Thompson presented his proposals to the Lindisfarne Fellows Conference for the design of a temple he called "the Grail," to be constructed in Colorado that would serve the same purpose as a *kiva* for mankind—a ceremonial semi-underground structure where the incarnation of Christ would occur.[28] Thompson called it a chapel in the earth.

The Lindisfarne Mountain Retreat was established and the Lindisfarne Fellows took up residence there, as did Gregory Bateson* (He died in 1980 at the Zen Center.), one of the founding fellows. Bateson was also affiliated with both the Easlen Institute and the Cathedral of St. John the Divine. He had been married to Margaret Mead for a while.

The temple was built for the Communion of the Mystical Body of Christ. The Lindisfarne Fellows believe the Grail is a meeting place between heaven and earth where humans communicate with "angelic" beings through deep group meditation—sort of an *antahkarana* or bridge between earth and the "Oversoul"—Lucifer. This is much like Findhorn, where "nature spirits" converse with the New Age occultists, and Lucifer appears in the form of the cloven-hoofed and horned god Pan.[29]

The Lindisfarne group fully expects to mate "God of the Heavens" (Father Sky) with "Gaia of the Earth" (Mother Earth) in the Grail. The goal: The Mystical Body of Christ through the union.

Invoking Father Sky

William Irwin Thompson writes about an attempt to invoke Father Sky into the Grail one day: "We all sat in silence, moving away from the peripheral noise . . . a circle was created among us, a vessel that could be filled with something else. One could feel the exact moment

---

*Gregory Bateson, a New Age psychiatrist and "consciousness" researcher, was instrumental in outlining the shape of the "new ecological consciousness."

that the vessel was formed, and then the moment there-
after when the power descended into the room."[30] He
then adds:

> In the intense experience of the . . . group medita-
> tion, I could see ourselves as the Grail, and yet at
> the same time, the whole planet as the Grail. The
> sun pouring light into the vessel of the earth was
> Christ as the solar logos pouring all his radiance
> into the earth and making all life possible. When
> in the future humanity [is] truly at one with itself
> and with the earth, then a new vessel of conscious
> evolution could be created, and into this vessel the
> Cosmic Christ would decend, and all humanity
> would become part of the universal Mystical Body
> of Christ.[31]

The Baca

"First, we want to bring all of the world religions
together and through that process bring some unity and
understanding amongst them"—Hanne Strong.[32]

The Baca at Crestone, Colorado, is the place where
Maurice Strong, the oil and steamship billionaire, and
his esoteric-oriented wife, Hanne, decided in 1978 to build
an international spiritual community—the "global village,"
they say—to accommodate the world religion. Many world
dignitaries have visited their Baca Grande Ranch in the
arid San Luis Valley, including Laurance S. Rockefeller,
the foreign minister of Zimbabwe, Henry Kissinger, Pierre
Trudeau, Robert McNamara, Robert O. Anderson, Amory
Lovins, the Dalai Lama, and some other members of the
Council of Foreign Relations and the Trilateral Commission not already mentioned. Shirley MacLaine has been
buying property nearby as well. The Baca is sixty miles
from the nearest supermarket in Alamosa and a day's
drive from larger cities.

During the last decade, the Strongs have donated six
hundred hectares and $1 million to various groups to
encourage them to settle in the Baca at the foot of the
Sangre de Cristo mountains. This United Nations proto-

type of spiritual beliefs include Hindus from India, Buddhists from Tibet and Japan, Catholic Carmelite monks, American Indians, and other assorted New Agers.

Lindisfarne Fellows

The Lindisfarne Fellows are involved with Zen group meditation and contemplation. They carry on Buddhist-Christian dialogue, give symposiums, publish materials, and generally attempt to globalize esoteric beliefs and practices. A primary goal is fostering "inner harmony of all the great universal religions and spiritual traditions."

Every spring they gather at the Cathedral in New York to review activities and make plans for the coming year. Each fall, Thompson serves as scholar-in-residence at the Cathedral and offers a series of public lectures or seminars, a public symposium (in collaboration with the Lindisfarne Fellows) on the exploration of "a planetary culture"—New World Order. Fritjof Capra, a New Age physicist, was one of the speakers in April of 1977, discussing "The Tao of Medicine." The Lindisfarne in Manhattan Program is funded by grants from The Lilly Endowment, the Rockefeller Brothers Fund, and the Rockefeller Foundation.

In true New Age fashion, the Fellows draw from Freemasonry, Theosophy, Alchemy, Hermeticism, Kabalism, Sufism, Ancient Egyptian, the teachings of Pythagoras, Neoplatonic schools, and even biblical text.[33]

Although the Lindisfarne Association is a "non-denominational and independent not-for-profit tax-exempt educational corporation," its headquarters are located in the Cathedral of St. John the Divine. "The Very Reverend" James Parks Morton serves as Lindisfarne's chairperson, and William Irwin Thompson serves as Lindisfarne's president and scholar-in-residence. Other colleagues from the Cathedral of St. John the Divine—Mary Catherine Bateson, John Todd, and Nancy Jack Todd—serve on Lindisfarne's board of directors.[34]

The Lindisfarne Mountain Retreat has transferred ownership of its eighty acres located in the Sangre de

Cristo mountains to the Dhrama Sangha of Santa Fe,
New Mexico. The Retreat is now called the Crestone
Mountain Zen Center and is under the direction of
Lindisfarne fellow and director Zentatsu Baker-Roshi.
That change should help to carry on the
Buddhist-Christian dialogue.

Lindisfarne began publishing in 1974 in collaboration with Harper & Row Publishers in New York. After
producing five books with that publisher and two more
with St. Martin's Press, the community at Southampton
moved to the Berkshire to establish the Lindisfarne Press
and has since published over forty books.

The Lindisfarne Association is named after the ancient Celtic monastery that was established on Holy Island in Northumbria in A.D. 635 and sees itself as a type
of change agent that will help bring about the transition
for the New World Order.

Gaia Institute

New York City environmentalists have, as the song
goes, found their paradise up on a roof. Biologists at the
Gaia Institute, located at the Cathedral of St. John the
Divine, are finalizing plans for a rooftop greenhouse and
recycling center that will turn a ton of food scraps and
yard waste into compost for a lush garden—using EPA
shredded styrofoam. The compost will be stored in hanging bins along the roof's walls and then drip into an
underground system that will feed the plants. Gaia Institute director Paul Mankiewicz figures his $450,000
Urban Rooftop Greenhouse Project will produce food to
be sold through the Cathedral shop and to neighborhood
stores and restaurants, with the possibility of becoming
a multibillion-dollar business if the idea catches on.[35]

Sounding like a lofty way to handle waste, this project
isn't the only thing the Gaia Institute has up its sleeve.
The theology behind the recycling project comes from the
"Gaia hypothesis," the pagan belief that the *earth is
alive*, a super-organism, and that all things must return
to the earth (a form of reincarnation). Founder of the

Institute is James Lovelock, British physicist and member of London's prestigious Royal Society, who has been battling for twenty years to spread his gospel of earth worship throughout the scientific community.

According to Lovelock's new book, *The Ages of Gaia: A Biography of our Living Planet*, the earth's physical features are its skeleton; the oceans, lakes, and rivers are its blood. The atmosphere is its breath. The brain, or collective consciousness, is the "thermostat" to regulate its body temperature—plants, animals, and humans (homo sapiens) included, are to work in concert as part of the ecosystem. All this, to keep the planet alive and well.

An environmentalist herself, Madeleine L'Engle sees the earth in much the same way. In her books, *Two-Part Invention* and *And It was Good*, she says, "We are one planet, a signal organism,"[36] "I'm not sure where the idea came from that all of creation is God's body, but if we must have an analogy, it is not a bad one."[37]

Scientists Mix Gaia and Politics

In March of 1988, the conservative American Geophysical Union* devoted a conference to Gaia.[38] While prominent researchers boycotted the meeting, some mainstream scientists found themselves considering the world as an "inter-dependent" planet.

Gaia Institute founder Lovelock has been given credit for developing New Age consciousness that stresses the unity of all things and manifests itself in ecological politics, holistic medicine, and art. In fact, in 1982, Joss Pearson founded Gaia Books, a London-based publishing house, to promote "the Gaian lifestyle." Its book, *Gaia:*

---

*Recently (during abnormally chilly June weather), the American Geophysical Union staunchly concluded that aerosols surround the planet and contribute to what some consider to be the "Greenhouse Effect," in spite of the fact that 81 percent of the scientific community says that global warming cannot be proven absolutely. It was the union's spokesman James Hanson who sparked public debate in 1988 by proclaiming that global warming had already begun.[39] Hanson's opinion provided the punch needed by environmental lobbies and green politicians to pass the Global Warming Bill.

An Atlas of Planet Management, featured contributions from more than one hundred scientists, naturalists, and public policy analysts from Cambridge, Oxford, Stanford, the World Bank, and the United Nations. Published by Doubleday, it has "produced a huge response among members of the Green Movement," the leftist environmental-political coalition that started in West Germany.[40]

Madeleine L'Engle's church, the Cathedral of St. John the Divine, is one of the centers of Gaia studies in the United States. "The Very Reverend" James Parks Morton gave a party for Lovelock in 1979 in honor of the publication of *Gaia: A New Look at Life on Earth* and has invited James Lovelock to preach there on more than one occasion. In 1983, the Gaia Institute was established, which offers study groups and workshops on Gaian principles, working with other Gaia groups and institutions around the world.[41]

More Gaian Supporters

IBM helped sponsor London's Commonwealth Institute, which in 1985 presented the Gaia hypothesis through a multimedia "scientific" and cultural exhibition called The Human Story. Among its offerings was a lively little pagan hymn entitled "Gaia Song," which went something like this: *"Gaia is the one who gives us birth / She's the air, she's the sea, Mother Earth / She's the creatures that crawl and swim and fly / She's the growing grass, she's you and I."*[42]

(L'Engle muses, "If we truly thought of the earth as Mother we could not do to her some of the things we have done.")[43]

Lovelock, a member of the druidic Lindisfarne association, is also an inventor who has supported himself from royalties from his many patents and scientific devices, as well as retainers from NASA, Hewlett-Packard, Shell, and other major corporations. It was Lovelock who invented the electron capture detector (1957), a palm-sized device that he created to prove that the chlorofluorocarbons (CFC's) were accumulating worldwide. His research was used in the worldwide environmental movement to ban fluorocarbon aerosols because of their "potential harm to the stratospheric ozone layer...." The still unproven theory has caused a controversy that continues to resurface.[44]

Much of Lovelock's work has been done in a laboratory, in his cabin located in a hamlet on the Cornwall-Devon border of southwestern England. It is there that a statue of Gaia, the earth goddess, graces his garden.

Gaia Institute and Something Fishy

According to their own publications, the Gaia Institute has its fingers in many pies, including an EPA-funded pilot recycling program, in partnership with the New York City Department of Sanitation, to convert waste to compost—to save space in landfills, they say. One building on each neighborhood block will be designated to have a giant "container system" in the basement, where waste will rot, then be picked up ten days later as compost by the city's newly designed and very expensive garbage trucks equipped with special "stealth" technology and functions.

Recycling and other earth-friendly programs, as everybody knows, is big business gaining public support and promotion. The media has been stiff-arming Americans, who as the "human species" have been made to feel guilty for simply being alive. It hardly seems appropriate, however, for a tax-exempt church to be going into a potentially lucrative business in partnership with New York City and the federal government, using our tax dollars as capital. Where will the profits go?

There's more. Gaia Institute is involved in the design of a wetland system for the Pelham Bay landfill, also under the consideration of New York City, planned to biochemically "melt down" the entire landfill in fifteen years, turning it into a park. The people in Schoharie and Orange counties in New York will be "blessed" with two waste/energy/agriculture demonstration systems designed to turn sewage into "fuel, food and drinkable water."

Gaia's publication also indicates that the Cathedral's
fourteen-story open space (the roof-top greenhouse and
recycling project) is being done in collaboration with the
EPA (your tax dollars at work) and uses the fertilizer
from the NYC sanitation program described above. As
the reincarnationists say, "What goes around comes
around."

The literature calls the Cathedral's swamp altar in
the nave of the building their "Earth Shrine," which
Gaia Institute describes as "a permanent exhibit of
Hudson River ecosystems." The philosophy of the Gaia
Institute is further revealed by their statement: "Most of
these projects work on several levels; practical and contemplative, or physical and metaphysical, or mechanical
and alchemical, or economic and spiritual." This certainly describes the yin and yang concept.

Children: Nature's Apprentices

Through environmental education curriculum, children are being introduced to earth stewardship, earth
monitoring, and earth religions, as well as learning what
the working class will have to do for the New World
Order—volunteerism and child labor! In New York City,
the Gaia Institute has devised a program to use public
school children from K-12 in a long-term ecological restoration project on the banks of the Bronx River, which
flows near the participating schools. Students will study
the history and ecology of the Bronx River Valley Watershed, monitor the site, and attempt to improve it under
the heading "Teaching Science through Ecological Restoration." The kids love the "take charge" curriculum and
field trips.

In a brochure called "Hands on Science along the
Bronx River: Apprenticeships in Ecological Transformation," we read, "The project was developed and will be
run by the Gaia Institute of the Cathedral of St. John the
Divine." Participating institutions are I.S. 167, P.S.6,
Monroe H.S. the Gaia Institute, Cathedral of St. John
the Divine; NYC Board of Education; Bronx River Resto-

ration; Bronx Council for Environmental Quality; NYC Department of Transportation; NYC Parks Department (Natural Resources Group); Metropolitan Life Insurance Co.; NYC Botanical Garden (Bronx Green-up Program); and Lehman College of CUNY.

Loudly Proclaimed Earth Summit

James Parks Morton's vision of a "spiritual U.N." is under way, thanks in part to oil billionaire and occultist Maurice Strong and the 1992 Brazil Earth Summit. Held at Rio de Janeiro, and attended by official delegates from 160 nations that included forty thousand environmentalists, industrial lobbyists, and activists of every stripe and color, the Earth Summit provided a forum for earth-friendly economists.

The secretary general and originator of the event—officially called the United Nations Conference on Environment and Development (UNCED)—was none other than Strong himself. He shares his friend Morton's vision of a spiritual and economic New World Order, governed by the United Nations.

In true inter-faith fashion, the Summit opened with prayers and invocations to God and demons alike. A variety of spiritualists invoked the goddess from the sea, prayed to the Buddhist Brahman, to themselves, and even to bananas and pineapples before eating them. Some illuminists even reflected the sun toward the conference with their pocket mirrors. About one thousand members from various women's groups from around the world, calling themselves the Female Planet, gathered at Leme Beach.

Global Forum 1992

While Earth Summit delegates were wrangling over proposed environmental treaties, Global Forum was holding its own Summit across the city in Flamingo Park for representatives of 250 non-government organizations (NGOs) and their individual activities.

Separate forums and exhibits were set up by religious organizations, Socialist movements, indigenous people's projects, monks, the Earth Parliament, the World Constitution and Parliament Association (WCPA), global educators, the Dalai Lama, former presidential hopeful Jerry Brown, St. John the Divine's James Parks Morton, U.S. Senator Al Gore, and former Prime Minister of Norway Gro Harlem Brundtland. Attendance numbered in the tens of thousands. As expected, world watchdog Ted Turner and his wife Jane Fonda were also there.

While all this was going on, *Gaia* arrived—a replica of a Viking ship, which was believed to have journeyed to America five hundred years before Christopher Columbus.

Attendees at the '92 Global Forum claimed that *millions* of pledges given to save the earth were sent by individuals from around the world. The pledges were attached to the "Tree of Life," which originated in the United Kingdom and was the main symbol of the convention.

In keeping with the theme of the summit, the Brazilian government had arranged to have thousands of homeless street people (mostly children) removed from public sight. And it even took steps to curb an outbreak of cholera among the poor, lest it spread to the conference attendees.

Earth Charter?

The twelve-day-long conference was expected to culminate in the ratification of an Earth Charter, a Bill of Rights for Mother Earth, that could cut across all other Bills of Rights and become the basis for *world law*. Instead, five international treaties and declarations were signed by 110 heads of state for "sustainable development" of the planet.

Included in these was a treaty drafted by 83 governments during a May 1992 conference held in Nairobi to save the earth's biological wealth—plants, animals, and microorganisms. This was one of the most important documents of the summit and could impact world economy. In addition, Strong said that "hundreds of thousands of U.S. residents will be asked to sign 'personal pledges of responsibility' for the planet's future."[45]

One of the more frightening creations of the Earth Summit was the Sustainable Development Commission, whose purpose is to police the world to assure compliance with the promises made at Rio de Janeiro (Rio), fostering new forms of global cooperation.

Richard Benedick, a state department negotiator, said, "The Rio conference is not a culmination. It's a step along a path that may continue. If the agreements reached in Rio lead to *new international laws*, the Earth Summit will have been a success."[46]

1995 Earth Charter

Both the governmental agencies and NGOs (non-governmental organizations) are now looking toward 1995, the 50th anniversary of the United Nations, as the next opportunity to declare implementation of their deadly Earth Charter. This gives them three more years at the drawing board. Earth-inspired NGOs are preparing for the next Summit with plans to permeate their theologies and philosophies in education, the churches, the arts, and business. We were told by one Rio delegate that when the time comes, the Earth Charter can be declared by a mass of people, and not just governments.

According to a World Goodwill report, Maurice Strong, the Earth Summit organizer, had considered the Earth Charter to be the most important outcome of UNCED (pronounced "un-said") 1992, calling it "a framework for behavior and action in the New Age."[47] Strong ended the Summit by threatening, "After the summit, the world will never be the same." The delegates cheered.

Champion for the Earth

Maurice Strong came to be known as the great-grandfather of the environmental movement some twenty years earlier, when he called forth the 1972 UN Conference on the Human Environment, held in Stockholm, putting ecology on the world's agenda. The meeting set up Strong's UN Environmental Program, and Strong was buoyed to a powerful position worldwide. That conference resulted in several governments creating their own environmental agencies. However, the big push for environmental rights came largely from radical ecology groups and Green parties in Western Europe and North America with close ties to the Socialist movement.[48]

Ironically, the earth's "great-grandfather" found himself in the middle of a couple of lawsuits for fraud—one in the Colorado courts. He was nailed trying to manipulate water rights away from the farmers.

Strong and his wife Hanne moved to Colorado from Canada in 1978 to take possession of a 160,000 acre ranch, where Hanne started her quest to turn the area into a New Age headquarters.* Strong and a group of investors took control of an oil exploration and livestock company called Arizona Land and Cattle (AZL). The property happened to sit atop one of the world's largest aquifers in the San Luis Valley of south-central Colorado.

In October 1985, Strong founded American Water Development, Inc. (AWDI), named himself president, and packed the board with luminaries such as Colorado governor Richard Lamm and former EPA head William

---

*Hanne Strong's vision for a world spiritual community at the Baca includes many representatives, groups, and individuals who have taken up residence there, including: the Spiritual Life Institute, a Catholic order of Carmelite monks; the Lindisfarne Association and educational retreat center; Colorado College (of the Aspen Institute for Humanistic Studies); the Haidakhan Samaji, a Hindu group; Sri Aurobindo and Savitri House Learning Center; Karma Triyana Dharmachakra, a Tibetan Buddhist organization; the Zen Institute of Japanese Culture; several Indian tribes; and Shirley MacLaine. Some twenty other religious groups and organizations are under consideration. Hanne Strong believes her grandson, Jason Mayo, to actually be Rechung Tulku, the reincarnation of an eleventh century Tibetan saint named Rechung Droje Drakpa. When he was four-years-old, Jason was formally enthroned in Tibet.[49]

Ruckelshaus. He then lobbied the valley residents to support his water rights application, telling them he would use the water for the valley. Strong was later exposed for planning to sell the water to Denver suburbs and elsewhere—a plan that would have realized $600 billion for AWDI.

Experts said the scheme of these wealthy "environmentalists" would have lowered the water level of the valuable aquifer to the point of turning the lush San Luis valley into a dust bowl—ecological devastation—as well as destroying the Great Sand Dunes National Park, located on the southern border of the Baca Ranch.

The citizens took AWDI to court and won; however, Strong and his group are appealing to the Colorado Supreme Court. Strong quit AWDI just two months prior to heading up the Rio Summit, claiming that his partners were greedy. He tried to give his shares in the company to the New Age Fetzer Foundation where, incidentally, he serves as a trustee. His partners retrieved Strong's shares instead, leaving him a tidy 2 percent share.

In Minnesota, Strong and AZL stockholders were sued for deliberately inflating the value of AZL stock. He and his co-defendants—including Adnan Kashoggi, the billionaire Saudi arms dealer—settled the suit out of court for $6.4 million.[50] So much for earth's great-grandfather.

Spiritual Leaders

The Dalai Lama's invitation to the Summit came from Global Forum, an affiliate of the Cathedral of St. John the Divine. Global Forum's satellite conference in Flamingo Park, at Rio de Janeiro, was attended by 7,892 non-governmental organizations from 167 countries. The event was described as "part New Age Carnival, part 1960s teach-in and part soap opera."[51]

It comes as no surprise that "The Very Reverend" James Parks Morton of the Cathedral of St. John the Divine happens to be co-director of the Global Forum. The board members include Buddhists, Christians, Hindus, Muslims, Jews, and a Jain Indian. Free for the asking, they sent out a slick brochure listing who's who at the Summit. Included were: Lucis Trust (formerly Lucifer Publishing), the Temple of Understanding, World Conference on Religion and Peace, World Council of Churches, Global Education Association, World Constitution and Parliament Association (with their World Constitution in hand for ratification), Wilderness Society, YWCA, Association of World Citizens (discussing a World Marshall Plan), Findhorn, Center for International Cooperation, Consortium on Religion and Ecology International, Greens in European Parliament, Global Tomorrow Coalition, International Academy of Environment, International Court of the Environment, International Youth and Student Movement for the United Nations, Kids for Saving the Earth (Target stores project), Meditation Groups Inc., New Ecological Socialism, Sacred Earth Network, Siera Club Legal Defense Fund, and Voice of the Children, among others.

CHAPTER SIX

000000000000000000000000000000000000000000000

Contemplative Prayer

"In contemplative prayer the saint . . . turns inwards in what is called 'the prayer of the heart,' not to find self, but to lose self in order to be found. We have been afraid of this kind of prayer, we of the twentieth-century Judeo-Christian tradition. . . . Why have we been afraid of it? Because it is death."

—Madeleine L'Engle, *Walking on Water*, p. 194.

Contemplative prayer—regardless of who practices it—is the universal concept of becoming totally silent, *of listening to "God."* Used by Buddhists monks, Rosicrucians, the early Church mystics, New Agers, and many Christians, contemplative or meditative prayer is a method of becoming deeply quiet and going into the "center of oneself, in order to merge with the divine." The "center" is an altered state of consciousness. "The divine" varies, according to one's belief.

The techniques used to get into this state are nearly always the same. Madeleine L'Engle describes this process in *And It was Good*, printed by Harold Shaw Publishers. She explains:

> The methods of contemplative prayer are similar in all traditions. Sit quietly, preferably comfortably . . . having found the physical context, breathe slowly, rhythmically, deeply. Fit the words of your mantra to this rhythm. And don't be afraid of the word, mantra.[1]

She then described one of her own meditations:

> One of my most-loved places for this kind of prayer
> is a large glacial rock on which I stretch out, flat
> on my back, so that I can feel that I am a part of
> the turning of the planet, so that rock and I merge,
> becoming part of the energy of creation.[2]

It is interesting that this same glacial rock (actually
located on L'Engle's property in northern Connecticut)
appears in her *Time Trilogy* and other novels. It is there
that the children meet their "angels," "teachers," Druids,
and other assorted demons for wisdom and instruction.

Contemplatives in the Church

Buddhist methods of meditation and contemplation
entered the Roman church hundreds of years ago through
its trade with Asian nations and pagan conquests, incorporating some of the strange religious traditions. Monasteries were established, where whole orders of monks
could study and practice the newly-discovered esoteric
traditions of these nations. Disciplinary methods of *self-
denial* were adopted from the eastern religions and developed into vows of poverty, chastity, and obedience—
traditions that have remained intact in monasteries and
convents throughout the centuries.[3]

Modern contemplatives, both Catholic and Protestant, seem to share a great reverence for those early
"mystics."

Seeking Spiritual Experiences

Rather than studying the Bible and submitting to the
inner work of the Holy Spirit, many Christians are fudg-
ing. They are looking to teachers, entertainers, books,
and seminars—looking outwardly for a new dimension
and level of spirituality. Some of their teachers are coming up with the message that "today's Church is missing
out on some wonderful spiritual experiences that can
only be found by studying and practicing the meditative
and contemplative lifestyle."[4]

Led by the rise in the popularity of the monastic lifestyle, contemplative prayer has found its way into the Christian community, providing instructions on "how to hear God's voice"—for those who are seeking "deeper truths." Proponents have even managed to come up with a biblical foundation for the quest: Adam and Eve *talked* with God in the Garden; Cain, Abel, Noah, Abraham, and the prophets all *heard* from God; and Paul was *taught* by the Lord Himself. Therefore, since Christ has been resurrected and has not stopped "speaking, teaching, and acting," then surely He communicates with His people today in an *audible voice*.

While seeking this "intimate relationship with God," many take up Zen meditation and its "spiritual disciplines" meditation, chanting, mantras, breathing techniques, visualization, and centering. However, Christian contemplatives tend to disguise the eastern practices by Christianizing them—like meditating on God's face, for instance.

Richard Foster: Contemplative Guru

Such a teacher is author and psychologist Richard Foster, a contemporary of Madeleine L'Engle, who was trained at George Fox College (Quaker). He served for a time as a professor of theology and writer-in-residence at Friends University in Wichita, Kansas. Recently, he has become "a distinguished professor at Azusa Pacific University in Southern California."[5]

Despite the biblical assertion that no one has seen God's face and lived, Foster takes his followers on spiritual journeys up beyond the heavenly places and into the "Presence of God," *face to face with the Creator of the universe* through the use of Eastern meditative techniques. His book, *Celebration of Discipline*, provides step-by-step instructions on how to: meditate, contemplate, "center-down (sit up straight, feet flat on the floor, palms up . . . palms down)," and "concentrate on the breathing." Using guided imagery, he leads his readers through the occult practices of visualization, meditation, and even astral travel. Even the *Witches Bible* describes astral travel as "the technique of shifting consciousness from the physical body and plane to the astral body and plane . . . It can be learned, or it can happen involuntarily. Such projection can happen when the physical body is very relaxed. . . ."

The following is an example of Foster's technique for "meditation" as found in *Celebration of Discipline.*

> In your imagination, picture yourself walking along a lovely forest path. . . . Try to feel the breeze upon your face as if it were gently blowing away all anxiety. . . . Walk out into the lush, large meadow encircled by stately pines. After exploring the meadow for a time, lie down on your back looking up at blue sky and white clouds. . . . [visualization]
>
> After a while there is a deep yearning within to go into the upper regions beyond the clouds. In your imagination allow your spiritual body, shining with light, to rise out of your physical body. Look back so that you can see yourself lying in the grass and reassure your body that you will return. Imagine your spiritual self, alive and vibrant, rising up through the clouds and into the stratosphere. Observe your physical body, the knoll, and the forest shrink as you leave the earth. Go deeper and deeper into outer space until there is nothing except the warm presence of the eternal Creator. Rest in His presence. Listen quietly, anticipating the unanticipated. Note carefully any instruction given. . . .[6]

At no time does this psychologist take the reader's spirit back into his body as he ends the visualization process. We do not believe in astral projection, simply because the Bible states that the body without the spirit is dead (James 2:26). Therefore, we believe out-of-body experience occurs within the mind itself. (Foster often uses music to aid these mind trips. A favorite chorus he gives his readers is "Set my spirit free that I might worship thee."[7])

It is no surprise that L'Engle enthusiastically endorses *Celebration of Discipline.* Like Foster, she believes "contemplation," or Eastern meditation, has great power and can facilitate astral projection. In *Walking on Water*, she wrote, "There are too many stories of mystics being able to move hundreds of miles through the power of contemplation for us to be able to toss them aside."[8]

Unfortunately, these practices are being widely taught to the general public today through cartoons, schools, universities, management retreats, seminars, etc. Often, the "unanticipated instructions," which come during such altered states, are actually demonic voices. By ignoring God's warning to repudiate the ungodly methods of pagans, many in the Church have fallen prey to these evil practices disguised as prayer. The following is a list of evangelicals who have unfortunately endorsed Richard Foster's teachings in *Spiritual Disciplines* (Second edition, pp. 203-210): Jamie Buckingham, former editor, *Buckingham Report*; Gary R. Collins, professor of psychology, Trinity Evangelical Divinity School; Tony Campolo, speaker and author, *Seven Deadly Sins*; Leighton Ford, Leighton Ford Ministries; William C. Fry, bishop, Episcopal Diocese of Colorado; Mark O. Hatfield, senator from Oregon; Caroline Koons, author, *Beyond Betrayal*; Judith C. Lechman, author, *Spirituality of Gentleness*; Madeleine L'Engle, author, *A Wrinkle in Time*; David L. McKenna, president, Asbury Theological Seminary; Calvin Miller, author, *The Singer* trilogy; John and Paula Sandford, authors, *Transformation of the Inner Man*; Luci Shaw, Harold Shaw Publishers, author, *Listen to the Green*; Ronald J. Sider, executive director, Evangelicals for Social Action; Lewis B. Smedes, author, *Caring & Commitment*; Howard A. Snyde, associate professor of church renewal, United Theological Seminary; Tommy Tyson, evangelist; C. Peter Wagner, professor of church growth, Fuller Theological Seminary; Robert Webber, professor of theology, Wheaton College; Macrina Wiederkehr, O.S.B., author, *A Tree Full of Angels*; Dallas Willard, author, *The Spirit of the Disciplines*; and John Wimber, pastor and founder, Vineyard Christian Fellowship.

(In the second edition of the book, the words, "We of the New Age," have been carefully changed to read, "We who follow Christ.")

Centering Down

Psychologist Richard Foster teaches that contemplative prayer requires "centering down," a New Age term that means to quiet the mind and body to complete silence and stillness. It is defined as re-creating silence . . . "re-collecting of ourselves until we are a unified whole . . . it is an active surrendering, a 'self abandonment to divine providence.'"[9]

In reality, it is a practice of shutting down one's mind to rational thought and opening it up to demonic influences and emotional responses. The Bible warns believers to be "sober-minded" and "vigilant," because our "enemy the devil prowls around like a roaring lion looking for someone to devour" (I Pet. 5:8).

Before Foster explains the centering down process, he issues some warnings. First, he explains, there's the problem of a wandering mind and "inner clatter"—type distractions that have to be quieted for "centering" to begin. Also, one must be careful not to fall asleep.* A third concern is more serious. Foster is a psychologist who has probably facilitated hundreds of meditations, yet he warns about the fear of spiritual dangers around meditative prayer—influences that are not of God. "It is a good fear to have, for Scripture is quite clear that there are Spiritual forces which wage against our soul. But the fear does not need to paralyze us, for 'greater is he who is in you than he who is in the world.'" He adds ". . . before every experience of meditation I pray this simple prayer of protection: 'I surround myself with the light of Christ, I cover myself with his blood, and I seal myself with his cross,' I know that when I do this no influence can harm me. . . ."[10]

---

*Falling asleep is common during meditation, because of the deep relaxation—otherwise, one goes into a trance.

Perhaps we should ask Mr. Foster why he dabbles in an area of spiritual darkness, where he feels the need to surround himself with protection? Conjuring up images and pictures in the imagination through centering is indeed dangerous!

Foster continues:

> Begin by seating yourself comfortably, and then deliberately let all tension and anxiety drop away. Become aware of God's presence in the room. Perhaps in your imagination you will want to visualize Christ seated in the chair across from you, for he is truly present . . . We might even want to visualize our bodies being lifted into the intense light of God's presence.[11]

Foster asserts that centering is necessary because God uses deep "centeredness," or altered states of consciousness, to "nudge us closer into the holy of holies." Once again, Foster is in direct opposition to the Word of God. At the moment of Christ's death on the cross, the curtain that separated the Holy of Holies from the world was rent in two, from top to bottom, a feat only God could accomplish. And it is through the shed blood of Christ that all true believers can march boldly before God's throne.

Emotional Popcorn

In *Meditative Prayer*, Foster takes his readers deeper and deeper into the "centering down" process, mixing hypnosis with suggestology, setting up the conditions for emotions to pop to the surface—a common occurrence in altered states. As he leads the readers through guided visualization into a relaxed, altered state, he begins to stir up their emotions and plants suggestions of "guilt" in the minds of the readers.

> A deep, godly sorrow wells up within for the sins of commission and of omissions . . . any deed or thought that cannot stand in the searching light of Christ becomes repulsive . . . [He takes readers on another visualization trip down a path of pebbles where we

see] our impatience, our nonacceptance give way
to a gentle receptiveness to divine breathings . . .
It's an entering into the rhythm of the Spirit.[12]

(In Zen Buddhism, "divine breathing" is known as
pranayama, Sanskrit for "controlling the vital life or
energy force.")

Rather than encouraging his listeners to be sensitive
to the conviction of the Holy Spirit, Foster actually cir-
cumvents this process by planting "triggers" in the mind—
key words, phrases, or symbols—that could spawn a re-
action in the future. As a psychologist, Foster should be
aware of the dangers of this form of hypnosis. God created man with a free will, and Christians should question any method that attempts to alter His purpose.

The Inner Personality

Foster teaches, "What happens in meditative prayer
is that we create the emotional and spiritual space which
allows Christ to construct an inner sanctuary in the
heart. . . . Meditative prayer opens the door. . . [to] transform the inner personality . . . the Divine Fire will con-
sume everything that is impure."[13]

God says just the opposite. According to Ephesians
2:8-9, there is nothing man can do to aid in his salvation.
We are dead in our sins, totally incapable of creating any
inner sanctuary for Christ. Nor does Christ need our
help to transform our minds.

Perhaps Christians should leave the responsibility
for conviction of sins where it belongs: with the Holy
Spirit, not with a hypnotist.

The Jesus Prayer

In keeping with the spirit of contemplatives, Richard
Foster obliges by providing a "mantra" for Christians in
Meditative Prayer. Mantras are often used to aid medita-
tors in reaching altered states of consciousness. Mantra
is a Sanskrit word meaning "sacred sound," and is a
sound, word, or phrase that is repeated over and over, to
impart power to the petitioner. Mantras have been used
for centuries in pagan cultures and were prevalent dur-

ing the early days of the church when God warned His people to avoid the "vain babblings" and "vain repetitions" of the heathens around them.

Reviving a practice of early mystics, Foster offers "The Jesus Prayer" to Christians to recite while swimming, jogging, or walking. It goes like this: "Lord Jesus Christ, Son of God, have mercy upon me."[14]

Madeleine L'Engle also promotes "The Jesus Prayer" as a mantra, stating that "it has great power." In *And It was Good*, she explains,

> Mantra is simply a convenient borrowed word for the kind of prayer that is constant. . . . For a Christian the mantra can be any short petition from the Bible, preferably one which includes the name of Jesus. The most frequently used petition is the cry of the blind man on the road to Jericho, "Lord Jesus, Son of the Living god, have mercy on me, a sinner," or a shorter version, "Lord Jesus Christ, have mercy on me."[15]

"The Jesus Prayer" is also recommended by people who do not necessarily identify themselves as Christians. New Age guru Ram Dass* says, "The use of a mantra sets up one thought, one wave, that repeats over and over again, dislodging your attachments to all other thoughts, until they are like birds gliding by." In other words, a mantra stops the thinking process. Dass also recommends "The Jesus Prayer," "Jesus Christ, have mercy on me," offering several variations from which one can choose.[16]

Another place we found "The Jesus Prayer" was in *The Mirror Mind* by Irish Jesuit William Johnston. The book was written as a creative approach to *self-realization*, mixing Eastern beliefs with Roman Catholicism. He

---

*Ram Dass is a New Age teacher, author, and guru. A primary promoter of the drug culture in the 1960s, Dass exchanged chemical dependencies for the brain's natural high—endorphins through deep meditation. He started the Hanuman Foundation, named for the Hindu monkey-headed deity, and has been on the board of directors for John Denver's New Age commune, "Windstar."

even quotes from a standard Buddhist dictionary to give
his philosophy a boost. Drawing upon the "great mystics,"
Johnston finds a way to incorporate Zen meditation and
"Christian" prayer, using God's name as a mantra. "Lord
Jesus, Son of God, have mercy on me a sinner."[17]

In December of 1989, the Associated Press printed an
article about the Vatican's warning to Catholics that
"such methods as Zen, yoga and Transcendental Meditation can 'degenerate into a cult of the body,' and it urged
proper Christian prayer." For the first time, the Vatican
had addressed publicly the problems raised by the "strong
attraction for some Catholics of methods inspired by
Eastern religions such as Hinduism and Buddhism,"
which involves prescribed postures and controlled breathing . . . "a quick way of finding God." Unfortunately, the
Vatican recommended the use of another mantra, "The
Jesus Prayer," to be done to natural breathing.[18]

Quietism

Contemplative prayer, like other forms of Eastern
meditation, contains elements of quietism. Quietism "de-
notes a heretical Christian movement, which came into
full flower in the 17th century in Spain, Italy, and especially France, although its roots stretched far back into
the past. The word can also be more generally applied to
any doctrine that denies the importance of the human
will in the attainment of perfection."[19]

At the foundation of quietism is the belief that unity
with God can only be attained through inaction, "through
a state of passivity so extreme that the soul itself is
annihilated; only so it can be reborn, and return to God."[20]
Like Foster, the Quaker, quietists believe that God can
be found within the center, the very depths of self—that
by stripping away the intellect, emotion, and personality, a person can reach a state of absolute nothingness.
At this point he can descend into himself, find the "chrysa-
lis of self," and become reunited with the Creator.

Quietism teaches simplicity and self-denial. The first
step on this path is a systematic exploration of one's

conscience, "an often giddy descent into self, to depths where the soul can rediscover its Creator."[21]

The second step is reaching a state of spiritual stillness, described as calm and peace. By doing this, the Quietist believes one fuses with God, and the soul takes part in God's perfection and remains there in paradise.

Most of the mystics quoted by L'Engle, Foster, and other proponents of contemplative prayer displayed elements of quietism, including Meister Eckhart, St. John of the Cross, St. Theresa of Avila, St. Francis de Sales,* and St. Clement.

Renovare

There is a "Quiet Revolution" coming upon the Church, according to Richard Foster. He identifies it as "the new move of the Spirit" and claims that out of it will come the greatest harvesting of souls in the history of the world. Foster sees Vineyard and Kansas City Fellowship, with whom he is in contact, as the greatest hope for what he called "this God-ordained Harvest."[22]

This "quiet revolution" might as well be called the "Quietist revolution," for it includes not only the promotion of the same esoteric practices found in Foster's books, but also a strategy for ecumenism, without regard to doctrine.

Renovare is the organization behind this movement, with an international outreach to those who are attracted to spiritual exercises not usually found in the local mainline church. Out of the traditions of Quakerism, Richard Foster and William L. Vaswig, co-directors of Renovare, are selling books and holding conferences for the "spiritually anemic," offering spiritual disciplines well-known to the pagan world to induce deeper spirituality. These include contemplative prayer, meditation, fasting, and study, which Foster calls the "Inward Disciplines." Fur-

---

*St. Frances de Sales—often quoted by Foster—carried quietism to the extreme place of self-denial. He reached the point of disregarding himself until hell became preferable.

ther, "Outward Disciplines" include simplicity, solitude, submission, and service, and "Corporate Disciplines" are confession, guidance, worship, and celebration.[23]

Purpose

Foster and Vaswig believe the Church is fragmented because of its spiritual anemia and has failed to reach its full potential. In an effort to mend the broken body and pull its pieces together, the two held Renovare's second National Conference on Personal Spiritual Renewal of Christian Leaders at Lake Avenue Congregational Church in Pasadena, California, on 23-26 October 1991. With more than one thousand pastors and leaders in attendance, the directors praised occultist/psychiatrist Carl Jung (see chapter 8) as a "great psychiatrist."

The conference "emphasized personal renewal through 'meditative prayer' involving 'centering down' to become quiet and passive, then used guided imagery and visualization of Christ."[24] These occult practices seem to be central to Renovare. Of course, both directors always deny that these practices are either New Age or occult.

Foster called for unity in the body of Christ through the "five streams of Christianity; the contemplative, holiness, charismatic, social justice and evangelical." Co-director Vaswig recalled that his first experience of "meditative prayer" using visualization was taught to him personally by Episcopalian mystic Agnes Sanford. He explained the contemplative aspect of Renovare's spiritual disciplines, the attainment of a state of mind that is totally passive and uncluttered by rational thought . . . the place where one can meet God, so Foster and Vaswig say. Practicing the "Presence of God" is actually a form of Zen Meditation.

Because of Foster's orientation as a psychologist, psychotherapy is woven into Renovare's methodologies (Media Spotlight, page 11) and into his books, *Celebration of Discipline* and *Meditative Prayer*.

In addition to conferences, Renovare has spiritual formation groups, associated with the Shalem Institute of Spiritual Formation, which practice a hybrid form of spiritual enlightenment, integrating Christianity and worldly philosophies. There, courses are taught that emphasize "Christian" contemplation and Tibetan Buddhist traditions, including breathwork, chanting, meditation, icon prayers, journaling, and reflection.

According to Al Dager's Special Report on Renovare: "It is little wonder that Foster, a Quaker, would institute such mystical practices [the doctrine of "nothingness"] in Renovare's curricula. The history and philosophy of Quakerism are marked by the mystical. Early Quakerism especially was given over to the inducement of trances, violent shaking (hence, the name 'Quakers'), glossolalia, visions and mindless ecstasy."[25]

Much of Richard Foster's life has been spent studying the mystics. Throughout his books, one can find numerous quotes from St. Francis de Sales (on developing the "senses"—an occult practice), Dietrich Bonhoeffer (on solitude and silence), St. Francis of Assissi, St. John of the Cross (dark night of the soul), Juliana of Norwich, Thomas Kelly, Morton Kelsey, Emmet Fox, Theresa of Avila, Evelyn Underhill (member of the Hermatic Order of the Golden Dawn), Thomas Merton, Meister Eckhart, Brother Lawrence, George Fox, Martin Buber (Jewish haisidic mysticism), Dag Hammerskjod (U.N. former Secretary General), and Frank Laubach (Wainwright House affiliate). Is it any wonder that he wrote, "We of the New Age can risk going against the tide"?

CHAPTER SEVEN

OOOOOOOOOOOOOOOOOOOOOOOOOOOOOOOOOOOOOOOOOOOOOO

The Chrysostom Society

Madeleine L'Engle is a member of a little-known contemporary Christian writers group called the Chrysostom Society. Each year this group of twenty "writers of faith" gather together in a different state to talk about writing, to share manuscripts and frustrations, and to collectively write. They also contribute articles for their official magazine, *Image: A Journal of the Arts and Religion*.

When the subject of the Chrysostom Society comes up, L'Engle explains that the group was started by Richard Foster, who convened a particular bunch of writers together. L'Engle says she "hotfooted" herself to Colorado, heading for the mountains.

Together, they had a lot of fun writing a serial murder mystery, called *Carnage at Christ Haven* (a Christian mountain retreat located near Florissant, Colorado). The book was published by Harper & Row, which also published Richard Foster's *Celebration of Discipline*. According to L'Engle, their next meeting was to be at Laity Lodge, a Baptist conference center outside Kerrville, Texas.

In 1990, the Society gave birth to a book called *Reality and the Vision*, printed by Word Publishing, which contains the insights of eighteen members of the guild. *Reality* pays tribute to each of the writers' mentors—those who most "stimulated their passion, and changed their lives in monumental ways."[1]

The editing task was given to Philip Yancy, former editor of *Campus Life* magazine, who now writes regularly as editor-at-large for *Christianity Today*. Yancy is advertised on the inside cover of the book as one of the "contemporary Christian authors" whose writings reflect "some of the most brilliant and creative work in the world."[2]

The Chrysostom Society was named for St. John Chrysostom, a fourth-century mystic who became the archbishop of Constantinople. He later came to be known by the Romans as the Church Father. The writers believe that his homilies were among the finest of ancient Christian writings, and the Society members now dutifully "pledge to carry on that tradition of excellence by encouraging one another to pursue the highest quality of writing possible."[3]

A look at St. John Chrysostom, the mystic, may help to understand the writings of the members of the Society that copped his name.

John Chrysostom (A.D. 347-407) studied at the distinctive School of Antioch (a school for monks) under a famous scholar, Diodore of Tarsus. Diodore had courageously defended the divinity of Christ against Julian the Apostate, the Roman emperor who attempted to revive paganism. During the same time, however, St. John also studied law under the famous *pagan* Sophist orator Libanius, "thereby illustrating the cross-fertilization of pagan and Christian cultures at this period."[4]

This marriage of the two religious philosophies of his day inspired him to join one of the loosely-knit communities of hermits among the mountains. He spent four years under the direction of a veteran Syrian monk and two years in a cave as a solitary. Because of ill health, he returned to Antioch, where he became an ordained deacon and priest before being appointed archbishop of Constantinople. Chrysostom, it is said, became one of the most accomplished "Christian" orators of his time and earned the title of "Golden-Mouthed." His sermons were eloquent and moving in his early years; however, his language became excessively violent and provocative as he grew older.[5]

In reading *Reality and the Vision*, we found members of the Society promoting paganism and Christianity. To illustrate this point, we have critiqued three chapters from the book.

Madeleine L'Engle

Society member Madeleine L'Engle chose to write about George MacDonald. L'Engle was introduced to MacDonald by her grandfather, who sent MacDonald's books from England. She claims her "mythic understanding" was deepened because of this author, and the "mythic world he offered . . . gave [her] solid ground" under her feet.[6]

However, George MacDonald's reputation rests on his fairy tales and his religious mysticism. He was ousted as a heretic from pastoring the Trinity Congregational Church after promising salvation to heathens and even animals. He also taught that hell was "but another facet of divine love which cleansed all sinners and prepared them for salvation."[7] While the Calvinists opposed him, he became more popular as a writer than he would have been as a non-conformist minister.

Like L'Engle, MacDonald frequently used familiar characters to tie groups of novels together, and his theology was laced throughout his writings. He believed in reincarnation—that "life is a dream and death is simply a walking into more life . . . death being only the outward form of birth." His concept of "resurrection" was mirrored in one of his *Lilith* heroes, Henry Vane, who moved between the seen and unseen worlds. After his wife's death in 1902, MacDonald lapsed into total silence and waited for "the death into new life," the reward he had promised his fictional heroes.

In her chapter on MacDonald, L'Engle voices her dissatisfaction with the Church today, using MacDonald's personal story as an example of unjust persecution, claiming the Church often accuses the innocent of heresy. She describes how she "fell breathlessly into one of the great pieces of religious writing" that spoke about "the great god Pan," and then adds:

> This, I am told, is now being labeled as "unChristian." Such blindness is sad indeed, and comes from a literalism which is unscriptural and judgmental and unloving. Am I being judgmental and unloving? I don't want to be, but I think there is a difference between judgment and judgmentalism, and I don't want fear of metaphor to deprive children of the awe and wonder with which we must all approach God.[8]

Since L'Engle continually boasts about her thorough research, it seems a little unusual that she wouldn't know that Pan is worshipped throughout witchcraft. Is she really calling the god Pan (Lucifer) a metaphor for Almighty God?

L'Engle also explains the special "gift" of "premonition" she has labored at since childhood, and which she discovered just prior to her grand-mother's death. L'Engle describes this as "second sight" or "previsions," stating that such gifts are consistent with the loving God (she calls him "El") that MacDonald had introduced her to. (According to the Psychic Dictionary, second sight is a form of clairvoyance or mental projection to the higher realms of the heavenlies.)

The works of George MacDonald are being given new life now. Bethany House Publishers has been gradually releasing newly edited versions of his longer novels. In addition, Harold Shaw Publishers has produced new editions of MacDonald's sermons.

Karen Mains

Karen Burton Mains, another member of the Chrysostom Society, chose to write about a true hero of modern times, Aleksandr Solzhenitsyn, whose toughness and perseverance in the face of the worst of adversity underscores his struggle in Russian labor camps.

However, Mains' chapter twists this man's genuine agony into what she calls a "mythological type of heroism." She lapses into esoteric jargon, quoting from an interview between occultist Joseph Campbell and Bill Moyers on the "Power of Myth." She praises Campbell for his emphasis upon mythical heroes and then redefines Solzhenitsyn's personal struggles, claiming he experienced a "transformation of consciousness . . . He loses himself for the sake of a higher end, undergoing a form of death and resurrection."[9]

It is deeply disturbing that Karen Mains would praise *The Power of Myth*, an interview in which Joseph Campbell blasted Christianity, the divinity of Jesus Christ, the inerrancy of Scripture, and everything Christians hold sacred—while at the same time speaking highly of human sacrifice, demonic possession, and other occult practices (see chapter 8). Here is a sampling of some of the statements Campbell made in his interview with Moyers:

> Jesus on the Cross, the Buddha under the tree, these are the same figures. . . . God is qualified as good. No, no! God is horrific! Any god who can invent hell is no candidate for the Salvation Army. . . . Heaven and Hell are within us, and all the gods are within us. This is the great realization of the Upanishads of India in the ninth century B.C. All the gods, all the heavens, all the worlds, are within us. . . . Ritual is group participation in the most hideous act, which is the act of life—namely killing and eating another living thing. We do it together, and this is the way life is.[10]

Throughout her chapter, Mains endorses other New Age ideas, such as Carl Jung's theory of the collective unconscious and an occultic *Time of Beginnings*.

> . . . the myths of ancient cultures vary; but their overall themes show an overwhelming similarity. . . . there is really only one story, translated in the traditions and circumstances of myriad people: the myth of a lost idyllic *Time of Beginnings* . . . "Doesn't this universal statement indicate a common collective memory of a paradisal time that did exist in actuality?"[11]

She then asks, "And, shouldn't we then cherish those rare few who can help us recover the buried memory, both individual and collective?"[12]

Why is this Christian writer promoting the concepts of an occult psychologist? Where is she getting this New Age heresy?

Karen Mains book, *The Key to an Open Heart*, reveals the source of some of this influence. Under the acknowledgments, she wrote, "I am grateful for the pioneering work of Agnes Sanford, on which much of the structure of this book is based." Agnes Sanford, an Episcopalian mystic and pantheist, is held in high regard by many New Agers. Sanford's book, *The Healing Gifts of the Spirit*, is even endorsed by *The American Theosophist*, the official magazine for members of the Theosophical Society in America, headquartered in Wheaton, Illinois.

In *Reality and the Vision*, Karen describes her personal collection of books that have gripped her "at a personal level," striking "a soulish satisfaction" in her. Among these is *The Chosen*, written by Chiam Potok, a Jewish mystic. Within this novel, Potok weaves elements of occult numerology, the Jewish books of mysticism, the Cabala, and the Zohar. (David Mains, Karen's husband, evidently shares her admiration for Potok. On his 1 July 1992 "Chapel of the Air" radio program, David called Potok one of his favorite authors and devoted an entire broadcast to *The Chosen*, never once referring to Scripture.)

Karen claims that her collection of books, some of which are "overtly Christian, others subtly spiritual," have a common "golden thread" binding them together: the "triune tuition"—"creation, fall and redemption."[13]

Karen and her husband, David Mains, co-host the daily national radio program, "The Chapel of the Air" from Wheaton, Illinois. Both write and lecture, and have been involved with the organization "Coalition on Revival." They also serve on Richard Foster's Renovare's Board of Reference. (Renovare provides teaching on contemplative prayer and Eastern forms of meditation complete with mantras.)

Richard Foster

Until recently, Richard Foster directed the Milton Center at Friends University in Wichita, Kansas, where he also served as professor of theology and writer in residence. He has written *Celebration of Discipline*, *Freedom of Simplicity*, *The Challenge of the Disciplined Life*, and *Meditative Prayer*. Foster is a founder and co-director of Renovare and founder of the Chrysostom Society.

For the Chrysostom Society book, *Reality and the Vision*, Foster chose the subject, "The Devotional Masters: A Love Affair," praising six authors who had changed his life—Dietrich Bonhoeffer, St. Augustine, Juliana of Norwich, St. Francis of Assisi, John Woolman, and Jean-Pierre de Caussade. Central to Foster's chapter is how the six writers individually influenced him in bringing about something he calls the transformation of his "inner personality." A few years ago, his basic opinion about society in general was that "superficiality is the curse of our age." So, in a spiritual trek to try to become less superficial, Foster sought something more. ". . . More of God, more of His love, more of His presence, more of His power." In his search, Foster turned to the mystics, the Devotional Masters, even though he admits some had "hare-brained ideas" and "inadequate theology" but "they learned to know God profoundly."[14]

Those two items should have made him suspicious. If one is going to seek out guides who can point the way to God, then solid biblical theology should be the first prerequisite. For to know God is to know His Word, which is where Foster should have gone.

According to Foster's chapter, Bonhoeffer showed him how preoccupied he was with himself and how to give to others. St. Augustine launched into a brilliant meditation upon pride, ambition, sensuality, laziness, prodigality, emulation, fear, and vengeance. Juliana of Norwich showed him the depths of Divine Love . . . of a somewhat sensual and "intimate" relationship with God. St. Francis of Assisi taught him a love for creation and "a merry abandonment to divine providence." Foster admits that he often finds himself chuckling and laughing, almost embarrassingly, but with what he calls "a deep resonant joy." John Woolman, a Quaker, alerted Foster to the social issues.

Says Foster, "I began my journey among the Devotional Masters out of desperation, but it has not ended there. Over the years desperation has turned to delight and delight has turned to a deep and abiding friendship—a love affair with the Masters. I invite you to join me."

The Society

Here is a partial list of the Society writers who contributed to *Reality and the Vision* and their literary masters and topics:

• Walter Wangerin, Jr.—Hans Christian Andersen: Shaping the Child's Universe
• Eugene H. Peterson—Fyodor Dostoevsky: God and Passion
• Robert Siegel—Musings: On a Life with Poetry
• Virginia Stem Owens—Soren Kierkegaard: Desperate Measures
• William Griffin—William Shakespeare: The Sweetest Prince of Them All
• Richard J. Foster—The Devotional Masters: A Love Affair
• Calvin Miller—Ray Bradbury: Hope in a Doubtful Age
• Emilie Griffin—John Milton: Sing Heavenly Muse
• Madeleine L'Engle—George MacDonald: Nourishment for a Private World
• John Leax—Thomas Merton: Giving Up Everything
• Larry and Carole Woiwode—Leo Tolstoy: Marching Straight at Truth
• J. Keith Miller—Paul Tournier: The Power of the Personal
• Karen Burton Mains—Aleksandr Solzhenitsyn: A Moral Vision

- Gregory Wolfe—Evelyn Waugh: Savage Indignation
- Philip Yancy—John Donne: As He Lay Dying

CHAPTER EIGHT

0000000000000000000000000000000000000000000000

Comrades and Affiliations

M. Scott Peck

Madeleine L'Engle and New Age psychologist M. Scott Peck (Scotty—as she calls him) are close friends and associates. It was L'Engle who encouraged him to branch out into fiction, a move that resulted in *A Bed by the Window*, his best selling mystery novel about sex and murder in a nursing home. (A reviewer for the *L.A. Times* "was appalled," claiming "the sex in this novel made my hair curl"; strange subject matter for a book Peck claims was inspired by God![1])

The Road Less Traveled, his first and most successful work (which he describes as a "solid New-Age book"[2]), brought Scott Peck national recognition and enthusiastic acceptance from both New Age and Christian communities. He is advertised in the *New Age Directory*, featured in institutes such as the Oasis Center in Chicago (where practicing occultist Jean Houston serves on the national advisory board), and has written for the *New Age Journal*. L'Engle also promotes Peck's books and views, even writing an endorsement (as did Marilyn Ferguson) for *The Different Drum*. In addition to sharing a common faith, they both are on the faculty of the Omega Institute, which specializes in courses on homosexuality, Zen, magic, witchcraft, altered states of consciousness, and various other occult arts.

Peck's endorsement by the New Age community is not surprising, however, in light of his doctrine; he espouses that ancient lie: *We are all gods*. He writes:

Since the unconscious is God all along, we may
further define the goal of spiritual growth to be the
attainment of godhood by the conscious self. It
is for the individual to become totally, wholly
God. . . . The point is to become God while preserving consciousness. . . .[3]

Peck then launches into a homily on the glorious
power and joy one feels upon reaching godhood:

The experience of spiritual power is basically a
joyful one. There is a joy that comes with
mastery. . . . we are participating in the omni-
science of God . . . Our conscious self has succeeded
in coming into alignment with the mind of God.
We know with God.[4]

He is quick to grab his "humble button," however,
adding that "those who have attained this stage of spiritual growth, this state of great awareness, are invariably
possessed by a joyful humility."[5] What arrogance! How
can any man claim to know God's mind?!

In a *Playboy* interview, he candidly shared his opin-
ions on such social topics as fidelity and pornography—
views which seem inconsistent for someone who is "becoming God." He said:

One of our myths is that we should be completely
happy with and fulfilled by one woman or one
man. . . . and that we should have no need to do
such things as look at pornography. That's nonsense . . . I believe pornography *can* be healthy.
Pornography can be used for good or for ill. . . . I
separate only the really demeaning, violent stuff.[5]

Otherwise, I think it's natural to look at pornography. I enjoy it.[6]

When the interviewer asked if such worldly views
had caused criticism, Peck commented that although
Christianity had for the most part "degenerated to a
bunch of magical hodgepodge,"[7] only the right-wing fringe
questioned his spirituality. He boasted, "People have
handed out leaflets saying that I'm the Antichrist. That's
power."[8] He went on to describe the depth of his own

morals and godliness. He did admit that having a "cult-like" following was tiresome, protesting that he did not want to be anyone's "f—— Messiah."[9] According to *Newsweek*, Scott Peck has a "propensity for four letter words" and Tanqueray martinis—his *Playboy* interview confirmed this.[10]

In light of such blatant blasphemy, it is distressing to see how Peck has been welcomed so readily into mainstream Christianity. If New Agers recognize Peck as one of their own, and if he is content to be so identified, then why can't Christians have the discernment to detect his heresy? Instead, he conducts seminars all over the world teaching Christian pastors his Zen methods of "community." Dr. Calvin Van Reken, assistant professor of moral theology at Calvin Seminary, recommended *The Road Less Traveled* in the 24 January 1992 issue of the campus periodical. David Mains spent several days reading from Peck's book, *The Different Drum: Community Making and Peace*, on nationwide broadcasts of "The Chapel of the Air." David Mains never told his listeners that Peck considers his books New Age or that *The Different Drum* promotes one-world government, mocks the sinlessness of Christ, and teaches Zen Buddhism. We wrote to the "Chapel" during the series of broadcasts, explaining Peck's New Age doctrines and affiliation, and enclosed a copy of his article from the *New Age Journal*. We were concerned that the "Chapel's" endorsement of Peck might lead many astray. Our letter was never acknowledged, and *The Different Drum* continued to be aired on their program.

When people ask Peck if he is born again, he jokingly responds, "If I am, it was a protracted labor and delivery."[11] When describing his "conversion" to "Christianity," Peck says he "became a Christian through twenty years of meandering through Zen, which is an ideal training in paradox. Without that training, there was no way I would have been prepared to swallow, ultimately, the god-awful paradoxes of Christianity . . . I found myself thirsting for a more fleshy, down-to-earth, carnal, bloody kind of religion. And of course, Christianity is the ultimately carnal religion . . ."[12]

Like L'Engle, Peck flatly denies the need for redemption, saying, "I worry about a theology that says that because this or that was done, that we've been saved."[13] Salvation, he claims, is found in ourselves, in "community," and is "a healing process of becoming whole or holy," of becoming gods.[14]

But Peck's heresy does not stop there. He joins L'Engle and other New Agers in denying the sinlessness of Jesus Christ. To illustrate this, he rewrote the biblical account of the Syrophoenician woman (Matt. 15:21-28) in *The Different Drum*. According to him, "Jesus recoiled in disgust" when the woman approached. Offended by her "atrocious accent . . . waves of fury filled Jesus. . . . He was tempted no longer to recoil but to jump forward and slap her, kick her, drive her away in his rage."[15]

Fortunately, according to Peck, Jesus was well- versed in the Zen tradition of "emptiness" and "meditation," which ultimately rescued Him from hideous prejudices and a violent temper. And David Mains read from this book over national radio. How can a Christian broadcaster give tacit endorsement to such heresy?

Peck also adopts L'Engle's New Age definition of the Second Coming, scorning Christ's promise that "I will come again and receive you unto myself" (John 14:3). While defining this concept, he wrote for the *New Age Journal*, "I am not talking about a bodily second coming. In fact, I am profoundly pessimistic about a church that would sit around passively waiting for its messiah to appear again in the flesh. Rather, I am talking about the resurrection of Christ's spirit which would occur in the church if Christians took him seriously."[16]

What makes that blasphemy worse is that he professes to be "called to write" by "the Holy Spirit . . . God."[17]

A leader in the disarmament movement, Peck advocates a "new American revolution" because the "institution of the presidency of the United States has become obsolete." As an alternative, he promotes a breaking down of "nationalism" and the founding of a "global community," a New World Order.[18] Pastors, beware. This concept of "global community" fulfills what is written in Revelation 13. . . . a future one-world economic community with a one-world religion.

Joseph Campbell

Joseph Campbell, the "Prophet of Myth," is highly regarded in New Age circles for popularizing a "mythical view of the universe," a belief that Madeleine L'Engle also supports. According to Campbell, all religions throughout history are simply different versions of universal myths. There is no such thing as spiritual truth or fact—everything is simply myth.

In 1986, shortly before his death, Joseph Campbell and Bill Moyers participated in an interview-format miniseries on public television called "The Power of Myth" (later published in book form),[19] which gave Campbell's philosophies and heresies coast-to-coast exposure. During this interview, Campbell promoted paganism and blasted everything Christianity represents. What was most striking were the similarities between many of his comments and Madeleine L'Engle's remarks in her "Wheaton Literary Series" produced by the Christian press, Harold Shaw Publishers.

For example, Campbell claims that Genesis contains two creation accounts—so does L'Engle. Campbell describes the God of the Old Testament as two gods: the loving Creator and the chauvinistic patriarchal god who promised the land of Canaan to Israel and condemned the pagan idolatry. This is also a constant theme in L'Engle's writings and lectures. Campbell goes even further, describing those who followed the true God during Old Testament times as members of an unfortunate cult!

> In the book of Kings and in Samuel . . . The various Hebrew kings were sacrificing on the mountaintops. And they did wrong in the sight of Yahweh. The Yahweh cult was a specific movement in the Hebrew community, which finally won. This was a pushing through of a certain temple-bound god against the nature cult, which was celebrated all over the place. And this imperialistic thrust of

a certain in-group culture is continued in the
West . . . We have today to learn to get back into
accord with the wisdom of nature and realize again
our brotherhood with the animals and with the
water and with the sea.[20]

He then embraces the gnostic view of Yahweh, our
God:

One problem with Yahweh, as they used to say in
the old Christian gnostic texts, is that he forgot he
was a metaphor. He thought he was a fact. And
when he said, "I am God," a voice was heard to say,
"You are mistaken, Samael." "Samael" means "blind
god:" blind to the Infinite Light of which he is a
local historical manifestation. This is known as
the blasphemy of Jehovah—that he thought he
was God.[21]

And what of Jesus Christ? Campbell said that Buddha and Jesus were the same person—they were both
manifestations of Christ. Like L'Engle and Peck, Joseph
Campbell flatly denies the sinlessness of Jesus, His virgin birth,* His unique divinity, His purpose, resurrection, and ascension. They both claim the death of Jesus
Christ was "not a ransom paid, or a penalty applied, but
that it was an act of atonement, *at-one-ment*, with the
race."[22]

Campbell dismissed the fact of original sin (as does
L'Engle in *A Ring of Endless Light*) and insisted that we
must free ourselves of the destructive myth of the Fall.
The biblical representation of the serpent as a seducer
was mocked as

a refusal to affirm life . . . The serpent represents
immortal energy and consciousness engaged in the
field of time, constantly throwing off death and
being born again. . . . Furthermore, the serpent
represents the primary function of life, mainly eat-

*Campbell compared the virgin birth of Jesus Christ to the mytho-
logical rape of Zeus and Leda—a theme developed in L'Engle's poem,
Bearer of Love, published by Harold Shaw Publishers in *Cry Like a
Bell*.

ing life. . . . The serpent . . . is the primary god, actually, in the Garden of Eden. Yahweh, the one who walks there in the cool of the evening, is just a visitor. The Garden is the serpent's place.[23]

Throughout the miniseries, Campbell condemned Christianity and the Bible as "based on a view of the universe that belongs to the first millennium B.C. It does not accord with our concept either of the universe or of the dignity of man. It belongs entirely somewhere else."[24] He described the human sacrifices of the Aztecs and then called Mexico City, where these incredible horrors occurred, a "sacred site"!

Like L'Engle, Campbell was greatly impressed by the ancient pagan goddess worship and by the "wisdom" of shamans. He explained that becoming a shaman required demonic possession and told how such possession was nurtured in certain Indian cultures. He describes watching a trance dance in which a man "experiences what we might call a possession" and then exclaims: "My God! This guy's had an experience of another whole realm of consciousness! In these experiences they are, as it were, flying through the air." *He then stated that the born-again experiences of Christians must be very similar to demonic possession!*[25]

Claiming that Jesus Christ was no longer a hero in today's culture, Campbell called for a new myth. "The only myth that is going to be worth thinking about in the immediate future is one that is talking about the planet."[26] And its symbol, he explained, should be a view of the earth as seen from space. This same symbol is used on the earth flag, which environmentalists have designed for the future one-world government. (The earth as seen from outer space on a dark background.)

Tragically, Karen Mains, co-host of "Chapel of the Air," praised the Campbell/Moyer interview in the book she co-authored, *Reality and the Vision*, published by the Chrysostom Society.[27]

Pierre Teilhard de Chardin

Mystic, paleontologist, Jesuit priest, and patron saint of the New Age, Pierre Teilhard de Chardin's writings laid the foundation for this movement. Teilhard sought to blend cosmic evolution with Christianity, a teaching that became the basis of his life's work. He resurrected the Nicolaitan concept of a "Cosmic Christ," Christ within all of creation—which has been described as a blending of pantheism and Christianity, or pan-Christicism—God in all of us. According to *Harper's Encyclopedia of Mystical and Paranormal Experience*, this was "one of Teilhard's greatest contributions . . . a shift from the dominant redemption orientation of Christianity to a creation orientation."[28]

Born in France in 1881, Teilhard was sent to a Jesuit boarding school at the age of ten. At eighteen he joined the Jesuit novitiate, and at twenty-four took a three-year post teaching in Cairo, Egypt. He participated in numerous expeditions, including the excavations of the "Peking Man" and "Piltdown Man," both of which were later determined to be frauds.

Impressed with Darwin's writing on biological evolution and Henri Bergson's philosophy of the evolution of human consciousness, Teilhard de Chardin chose to redefine Christian theology incorporating these theories. His absolute acceptance of evolution, however, drew censure from the scientific community, who criticized him for treating evolution as a dogma and not a hypothesis. Evolution is the ultimate foundation upon which *all* Teilhard's conclusions stand.[29]

Although the press and educational system would have the public believe that all scientists have accepted evolution as fact, this is not the case. At the Darwin Centennial, many scientists revealed their doubts about evolution and their dissatisfaction with Teilhard's treatment of this untested, unproven theory. Dr. Hans Gaffron was among those who opposed:

"There is a nice theory, but no shred of evidence, no single fact whatever, forces us to believe in it. What exists is only the scientists' wish not to admit a discontinuity in nature and not to assume a creative act forever beyond comprehension."[30]

Everett C. Olson, who works in the field of evolution, participated in the Darwin Centennial and commented that numerous scientists, including biologists and paleontologists, actually believe that current evolutionary theories are false.[31]

Another incident, which damaged Teilhard's credibility as a scientist, was his involvement in the Piltdown scandal. In 1912, outside Piltdown, England, Charles Dawson and Arthur Keith discovered a so-called "apeman," a missing link in the chain of evolution. Teilhard de Chardin and Sir Arthur Woodward came to assist in the work. For forty-one years, the "Piltdown Man" was displayed in the British Museum as positive proof of evolution. In 1953 (two years before Teilhard's death), scientists John Winer and Samuel Oakley discovered that "Piltdown Man" was an intentional hoax! Through careful examination, they found that the skull was a modern man, the jawbone was from an ape, and human teeth had been filed deliberately to look as if they belonged to an ape. Additionally, the jawbone had been treated with bichromate of potassium and iron salt to appear fossilized.[32] It only seems logical to question the theology of a man who would participate in such a fraud to support his beliefs.

Teilhard perceived the cosmic evolution of man as a four-stage process of becoming human. The first stage, the "lithosphere," involved the progression of inorganic matter; next came the "biosphere," or appearance of living forms. Life somehow progressed into human form, and with the introduction of human consciousness, the "noosphere" began, and man became responsible for his own evolution. According to Teilhard, man must consciously co-create with God, furthering his own evolution with intentional acts, always striving for the final stage, the Omega point, when the individual ceases to exist as a part of the Cosmic Christ. Teilhard titled this process "Christification," and called for a conspiracy of people who would strive to push mankind to this final step of evolution, becoming gods. The New Age movement is the answer to that call.

Because of the heretical nature of his doctrine, the Jesuits would not allow him to publish his works. Ironically, it was the Jesuits who published Teilhard's books after his death, which have now sold in the millions and are available in almost every language. New Age proponents have enthusiastically embraced the teachings of this priest. Madeleine L'Engle tells of reading Teilhard de Chardin's books and being "fascinated by his loving theology,"[33] and evidence of his theology permeates her writings. In *Stone for a Pillow*, she blasts those who expose the heresy in this man's teachings.[34]

New Age spokesperson Marilyn Ferguson credits Teilhard with inspiring the name "Aquarian Conspiracy," and weaves his teachings throughout the fabric of her book.[35] In fact, she claims that Teilhard de Chardin "was the individual most often named as a profound influence by the Aquarian Conspirators who responded to a survey."[36]

In 1967, Barbara Marx Hubbard was so influenced by Teilhard's concept of transcendent consciousness that she invited a thousand people who shared this belief to join her in creating a "human front." Thomas Merton was among the hundreds who responded to her invitation. Their loose-knit organization became known as the New Age "Committee for the Future."[37]

Mundelein College

"The two colleges where I feel most at home, and where I have been going regularly for the past decade [since the early 1970s], are Mundelein, in Chicago, which is Roman Catholic, and Wheaton, less than an hour away, which is Evangelical. You'd think they'd be about as far apart as Christians can get, but I feel equally at home and befriended in both places."—Madeleine L'Engle, *Walking on Water*, p. 148.

Mundelein College in Chicago, which L'Engle regards as a home away from home, has drawn censure from

many within the Roman Catholic church for its bizarre
ceremonies and pagan curriculum. The college seems to
share L'Engle's fondness for ancient goddesses, which
they display with celebrations such as "The Goddesses
and the Wild Woman," held on its campus in 1985. It was
sponsored by the Chicago Call to Action and the women's
issues committee of Mundelein's graduate program of
religious studies.

> The event's brochure shows what is apparently a
> woman dancing in the Vedic fashion, one breast
> exposed, flowers springing from her steps, the new
> moon on her cloak and catching a star in what is
> a magic wand. . . . A chorus of ancient goddesses
> stand by—Demeter the earth mother, holding
> Persephone in her arms Madonna-like; Hestia,
> mistress of the Vestal Virgins; the moon-goddess
> Artemis, Aphrodite, the goddess of love, who
> emerged from sea foam and is circled with a love
> compelling girdle; Pallas Athene, who sprang full-
> armed from the head of Jupiter; and Hera, wife of
> Jupiter, queen of the gods. . . . these divinities
> seem to have found welcome in Chicago.[38]

Other questionable activities that have been held at
Mundelein include seminars that teach gnosticism and
New Age courses such as "Discipleship for a New Age,"
"Wholistic Spirituality for a New Day," and "Sexuality in
a New Age." Perhaps it was because of this pagan cli-
mate that Matthew Fox, a Dominican priest and self-
proclaimed New Ager, chose Mundelein College as the
place to start his Institute of Culture and Creation Spirituality (ICCS). These events occurred, incidentally, after
L'Engle began visiting Mundelein regularly.

Through the ICCS, the college offered Master of Arts
degrees in culture and spirituality, creation spirituality
and geo-justice, and creation spirituality and psychology.
These degrees continued to be offered even after Fox and
the ICCS staff moved to Holy Names College in Oakland,
California, in 1983.

Matthew Fox

Among the ICCS instructors hand-picked by Matthew Fox to preach his pagan religion of creation spirituality are a masseuse; a Zen Buddhist; instructors in martial arts and yoga; an African priestess of Oshun; Buck Ghost Horse, an instructor in Native American religion; and his close personal friend, Starhawk, a priestess of Wicca (witchcraft), who teaches a course on rituals.[39]

Miriam Starhawk is best known for her occult book *The Spiral Dance*, a training manual for performing rituals such as "casting the circle, raising the cone of power, invoking the Goddess and God, and reaching trance states. The book also gives spells, chants, invocations, and advice on creating one's own rites."[40] In addition to teaching at Mundelein College and now at Holy Names College, Starhawk has founded two covens in San Francisco, is a licensed minister of the Covenant of the Goddess, and has written film scripts, articles, and poetry.

> Matthew Fox refers to Starhawk as a "scholar of the goddess religion called Wicca whose magic is a spiritual path." This is a "tried and true method of non-egocentric self-realization and community building . . . a practice of awakening and acknowledging the Divine Power within each of us."[41]

Starhawk ends her lectures with a ritual called the Spiral Dance, which includes a chant, "Earth, wind, fire, spirit, return, return, return." As the dance ends, many of the participants kneel or sprawl upon the ground, worshipping Goddess Earth.[42] It is interesting that Matthew Fox also uses this ritual in the climax of his Creation Spirituality seminars. One of the writers attended a workshop given by Fox at the First Congregational United Church of Christ in Longmont, Colorado, on 7 March 1987.* He closed his lecture by taking partici-

---

*The First Congregational United Church of Christ has also featured such speakers as: John A. Sanford, Howard Thurman, James Pike, M. Scott Peck, Sidney Harris, and Elisabeth Kubler-Ross.

pants out onto the church lawn and leading them in one of the oldest witch dances, the same spiral dance that Miriam Starhawk teaches. With Fox as a leader, the participants formed a human chain, holding hands while he led them into a spiral, chanting "Earth, wind, fire, spirit, return, return, return." At the end of the dance, he said, "Let us all worship the goddess to whom we belong." At this point, they all fell down, worshipping the earth, some on their faces, others on hands and knees.

Matthew Fox has spread his heretical New Age doctrines through a number of books, including: *Manifesto! For a Global Civilization*, which advocates a one-world government and one-world religion and a pantheistic view of God; *The Coming of the Cosmic Christ*, which bears an endorsement by M. Scott Peck on the back cover; *Whee, Wee, We All the Way Home; Western Spirituality; Meditations with Meister Eckhart* (with whom he claims to communicate in a fashion similar to L'Engle's method of kything[43]); *Original Blessing: A Primer in Creation Spirituality*; and *The Illuminations of Hildegard of Bingen*.

Fox shares many common beliefs with L'Engle, Peck, Joseph Campbell, and other New Agers. These include monism—the belief that God is not a separate force, but an integral part of all created matter; pantheism—identifying God with the forces of nature; feminist spirituality—a view of God as female, a return to pagan goddess worship; creation spirituality—the sacredness of all creation; divinity of man—the old lie that we are all gods; and a bizarre belief that all life feeds on life—that we live by killing. This view comes from seeing every animal, gnat, fruit, vegetable, and blade of grass as possessing a spirit. At his workshop at the First Congregational United Church of Christ in Longmont, Colorado, Fox stated, "Life is about killing and being killed, eating and drinking the cosmic Christ. We need to celebrate this killing."

Morton Kelsey

Episcopal priest, writer, lecturer, and Jungian analyst Morton Kelsey has been instrumental in bringing occult practices into the church. Early in his ministry, Kelsey was profoundly influenced by the Episcopal healer and writer Agnes Sanford and by his Jungian analyst, Max Zeller. He became so impressed with the teachings of Carl Jung that, after he finished his therapy with Zeller, he flew off to the Jung Institute in Zurich for three months. At the clinic, Kelsey and Jung began a relationship that they developed over the years through correspondence.[44]

Kelsey boldly states, "You can find most of the New Age practices in the depth of Christianity," and then urges Christians to adopt ESP, telepathy, altered states, out-of-body experiences, clairvoyance, and other occult arts. These gifts, he claims, need to "be understood as natural and morally neutral. Like the gift of a great singing voice or an ability to make money, it may be used for good or for evil, *for God or the evil One*."[45] His book, *The Christian and the Supernatural* (which reads like a primer for witchcraft), attempts to prove this hypothesis, instructing Christians on tapping into the powers of the occult. To support his belief in paranormal experiences, he draws from such occult sources as *Shamanism, The Teachings of Don Juan*, and *I Ching*—even claiming "there are few more interesting or profound books than the *I Ching*."[46]

Kelsey teaches the effective way to reach the psychic realm through altered states of consciousness. His book describes six ways of reaching an altered state: dreams, meditation and religious rituals, trance, hypnotic trance, hallucinogenic drugs, and through indirect methods such as using ouija boards, mediums, and automatic writing, a form of channeling.[47] Like L'Engle, Kelsey recommends keeping a dream diary and using mandalas and mantras such as the Jesus prayer to effectively reach another reality, the "other side of silence."

Morton Kelsey echoes the warnings of other occultists that there are certain dangers in these practices. For

example, Kelsey endorses the use of hallucinogenic drugs
such as peyote but cautions that "the use needs to be
surrounded by ritual and contained" to prevent encoun-
tering evil spirits or becoming addicted.[48] Witches cast
spells to protect themselves from evil during rituals in
their ceremonies for the very same reason. While ac-
knowledging that there is some inherent danger in drug
use, Kelsey argues:

> The subject of drug use arouses so much emotion
> that it is difficult to talk about it objectively. . . .
> Drugs can be used to get into another realm or
> world and so to widen one's experience of reality or
> state of consciousness. This use, although poten-
> tially dangerous, is not essentially a mechanism of
> mental illness as much as an effort to experiment
> with altered states of consciousness. It represents
> an attempt to expand experience rather than to
> retreat from reality.[49]

The blame for the worldwide misuse of drugs, he
contends, lies with the Christian Church. By forbidding
occult practices, Christianity has robbed its followers of
legitimate methods of reaching altered states of consciousness. If the Church wishes to combat the problem
of drug abuse, he says, then it must provide Christians
with its own ways of reaching the same altered states
through "mystical experience, imaginative meditation,
and various encounters with more than the physical
world."[50]

Kelsey describes automatic writing or channeling as
a fascinating way of touching the spirit realm. *The Seth
Material* and *Seth Speaks*, two books channeled through
Jane Roberts by a demon who calls himself Seth, are
recommended as good examples of this form of psychic
contact, which serve to validate the human soul. Regarding other channeled materials, he writes, "Although some
of these writings seem to have been inspired by rather
shallow spirits, other such works show true creativity."[51]

This Episcopal priest recommends occult practices
such as transcendental meditation (TM), Zen, yoga,
mandala contemplation, sensory deprivation, biofeedback,

mantras, and shamanism as good training exercises for Christians

> in reaching stillness and opening themselves to new experiences within. . . . There is real danger in much of Eastern thought and in our own scientific probing into the mind, but it is not because there is something dark and evil lurking in either of them. The danger lies in the fact the Eastern ways of prayer and scientific interest in altered states of consciousness do not go far enough . . . [this] is only the first step on the journey of meditation.[52]

Kelsey's book, *The Other Side of Silence*, was written to take the Christian all the way down this path of occult meditation.

It is interesting that L'Engle claims to write from this "other side of silence," where she taps into the collective consciousness. Perhaps because of the similarity in their doctrines, Kelsey recommends Madeleine L'Engle's book, *The Irrational Season*, in his own book, *Caring*.

When asked by a reviewer which Christian organizations best encompass Kelsey's view of spirituality, he recommended the Presbyterian San Francisco Theological Seminary's Center for Spiritual Discipline; Washington, DC's Church of the Savior; and a religious retreat in Pennsylvania named Kirkridge, praising it for its effort to bring a "religious dimension to different aspects of human life."[53]

Kirkridge

Kirkridge Retreat and Study Center opened in 1942 as a refuge for "pilgrims seeking solitude and community, rest and discernment, toward personal and social transformation."[54] Founded by John Oliver Nelson, a Presbyterian minister, Kirkridge is located on two hundred and seventy acres of Pennsylvania Appalachian mountain property.

According to their catalogue, the purpose of the center is the "integration of personal growth and social change," which they seek to accomplish through a wide range of religious expressions. Here is a sample of the interesting assortment offered in Kirkridge's 1992 spring and summer schedule.

"A Retreat with Madeleine L'Engle"—a weekend of readings and conversations with Madeleine L'Engle including matters of spiritual life and her personal theology.

"The Dancing Warrior"—a dance course designed to unite the body and spirit through Spiral Dance, Ki Breathing, the Circle, Dance Power and Presence, and martial arts. The course blends the Lakota Sioux tradition of the "Spiritual Warrior" with other pagan traditions. Activities include building a Sweat Lodge.

"Spring Sabbath"—an exercise in quietism, seeking a rhythm of "moving inward, moving outward," exploring the "gifts of quietness." Through contemplative silence, the participants "enter the mystery of the Sabbath (the sanctity of time) and Sanctuary (the sanctity of space) within us."

"The Ecology Crisis and Creation Mysticism"—taught by none other than Matthew Fox, a workshop that explores ecology through creation mysticism. Fox promised to lead the participants through meditation experiences, dance, and a cosmic liturgy on Sunday morning—to better prepare the participants for the coming "paradigm shift to a new cosmology."

"Meeting the Shadow"—a course taught by Jungian therapist and dream analyst, Jeremiah Abrams. Abrams is the editor of *Reclaiming the Inner Child* and co-editor of *Meeting the Shadow: The Hidden Power of the Dark Side of Human Nature*. The course was inspired by Carl Jung's suggestion that each person discover a deeper source of spiritual life through "shadowwork." To do this, he (Jung) said, we are "obliged to struggle with evil, to confront the shadow, *to integrate the devil. There is no other choice.*" The brochure explains that the course helps people to

> become whole. By making conscious and integrat-
> ing the shadow, we gain access to the treasure
> store within: behind the dark aspect that it repre-

sents, there stands the aspect of wholeness. The shadow is the keeper of the gate, the guardian of the threshold. Befriending the shadow allows us to gain the friendship of the self.

"Gay/Lesbian and Christian: Called to Love"—the sixteenth annual gay/lesbian retreat to be held at Kirkridge a celebration of homosexual lifestyles. Each year the participants build a gay/lesbian church on the mountain. One of the instructors was Virginia Ramey Mollenkott, English literature professor at William Paterson College and author of *The Divine Feminine*.

"Summer Sabbath"—led by Edwin Beers, a United Church of Christ clergyman, offering another exercise in quietism. The "gathering" emphasized silence and solitude, incorporating prayer, meditation, monastic simplicity, yoga, and movement.

"The Spirituality of Thomas Merton"—a retreat exploring the theology and biography of mystical priest Thomas Merton.

Fritjof Capra

Fritjof Capra, physicist, author, and self-professing New Ager, is best known for his book, *The Tao of Physics*, which blends the Eastern mystic traditions of Hinduism, Buddhism, and Taoism with "new physics." Capra was inspired to write this book while in an "altered state" of consciousness.

> I was sitting by the ocean one late summer afternoon, watching the waves rolling in and feeling the rhythm of my breathing, when I suddenly became aware of my whole environment as being engaged in a gigantic cosmic dance . . . I "saw" cascades of energy coming down from outer space, in which particles were created and destroyed in rhythmic pulses; I "saw" the atoms of the elements and those of my body participating in this cosmic dance of energy; I felt its rhythm and I "heard" its sound, and at that moment I knew that this was the Dance of Shiva, the Lord of Dancers worshipped by the Hindus.[55]

This drug-induced "experience" was followed by many similar episodes that he claimed convinced him of the "truth" of modern physics and "ancient Eastern wisdom."[56] The influence of "outside power" was so strong that Capra said "sometimes, while writing *The Tao of Physics*, I even felt that it was being written through me, rather than by me. The subsequent events have confirmed these feelings."[57]

Capra found it difficult to enter "altered states" through meditation alone during the early years of his mystical training, so he used drugs. Of his trips, he admits, "In the beginning, I was helped on my way by 'power plants' which showed me how the mind can flow freely; how spiritual insights came on their own, without any effort, emerging from the depths of consciousness."[58] These "power plants" are actually hallucingenic plants, such as poppies (which L'Engle used in childhood to enhance her dreams), psychedelic mushrooms, and other drugs.

Drugs are often used by people interested in reaching "altered states of consciousness." The ultimate goal of Eastern meditation is training the mind to trance using one's natural brain chemistry. Through meditation techniques, the devotee learns to release endorphins, natural pain killers in the brain, which have a morphine-like effect in the bloodstream. The resulting experience can be compared to taking LSD or any other hallucinogenic drug. This is the reason Episcopal Bishop Morton Kelsey claims he recommends teaching people meditation—so they can have the same experiences they receive from drugs, supposedly without physical harm. The full effects of the unnatural endorphin release is not actually known, but one can become psychologically addicted to this meditative process because of the euphoric high that is experienced. "Tripping out" through meditation can open up a whole world of demonic influence.

It's difficult to understand why anyone would give much credence to "scientific knowledge" revealed through drug-induced states, yet many believe this mystical interpretation of physics. Madeleine L'Engle endorses *The*

Tao of Physics in her autobiographies. In fact, Capra's teachings of the mystical "interdependence of all matter" are woven throughout L'Engle's book *And It Was Good*.

Like L'Engle, Capra is also an avid environmentalist, supporting a one-world community. In *The Turning Point*, he discusses what is required to create a "sustainable society" if planet Earth is to survive. What he describes is a socialistic, totalitarian government, which would require forced birth control, dictate where a person would work and live, remove vehicles and other forms of modern transportation from all but a chosen few, and even control what people would be allowed to eat. It is the removal of all the personal liberties enjoyed in free countries today.

According to Capra, one of the best vehicles for making necessary changes is the Green Party. In the book, *Green Politics*, Capra and co-author Charlene Spretnak describe the rise of the Green Party from its neo-Nazi origins in West Germany—where it is now that country's most powerful political party—and promotes the party's ecologically-based social agenda. Though the Green Party is much stronger in Europe than in the United States, its influence in America is astounding, beginning with Earth Day.

Fritjof Capra is also on the International Council of the Global Education Association (GEA), whose stated agenda is the development of a global society, which would replace individual nation-states.[59] The GEA took an active part in composing the Earth Covenant. The Covenant was presented in the 1992 Earth Summit.[60] He has participated in the Lindisfarne in Manhattan Program at the Cathedral of St. John the Divine.

Thomas Berry

Thomas Berry is a New Age Catholic priest who calls himself a "Geologian"—a theologian of the earth. A member of the advisory boards for the Global Education Associates and the Temple of Understanding, Berry is also a frequent speaker at Madeleine L'Engle's church, the Cathedral of St. John the Divine. Deeply influenced by

Teilhard de Chardin, Berry served as president of the American Teilhard Association. He has also been a chaplain with NATO in West Germany, taught Chinese and Indian history, and studied Native American religions. He now heads New York's Riverdale Center for Religious Research.

Sharing a view held by Matthew Fox, Madeleine L'Engle, Joseph Campbell, and others, Thomas Berry places the blame for environmental ills squarely on the shoulders of Christianity. It is the "myth" of Genesis—that man is a unique creation separate from nature—which will lead us to "environmental Armagaddon," he claims. The only way to avoid such a fate is to adopt a "New Story," or "new Myth," "one that celebrates the sacredness of all the universe as well as our interdependence with it."[61]

His collection of essays, *The Dream of the Earth*, offers "nothing less than a blueprint for reinhabiting the Earth in a way that reflects our cosmic interdependence." Accomplishing this, he writes, would require replacing democracy with "biocracy" and establishing "bioregions, geographic zones that are both self-governing and self-sufficient."[62] These zones would be answerable to a higher ecological governing power, replacing existing governments—and the United States Constitution as well.

Carl G. Jung

One of the common threads tying Madeleine L'Engle and other New Age adherents together is a cult-like reverence for psychiatrist Carl G. Jung. L'Engle quotes from Jung extensively in her books and lectures.

As a child, Jung began a life-long fascination with the occult, and this unholy preoccupation permeated his work. Personally tutored by Sigmund Freud, Jung parted ways with his mentor as he began to formulate his own view of psychiatry. Jung rejected Freud's idea that all behavior was governed by sexual drives and developed his own school of thought.

According to Jung, there exists a great pool of knowledge and psychic experience—the collective unconscious—

which contains archetypes, or character patterns, that direct our behavior. The goal of psychoanalysis, he claimed, was to teach people how to tap into this "vast storehouse" of knowledge. Much of the inspiration for this theory came from studies Jung had done on people who had experienced psychic phenomena and demonic encounters. He also claimed to have received insight about the collective unconscious and other mysteries from numerous spirit-guides (demons), including one who claimed to be an ancient Gnostic named Philemon. Jung described Philemon as a wise old man "with a long white beard, the horns of a bull, and the wings of a king-fisher."[63] It's no wonder that Jung's theology often resembles other works, such as *A Course in Miracles* and *The Lost Teachings of Jesus*, which are also channeled by spirit-guides.

Adopting a monistic/pantheistic view, Jung taught that God was not a separate entity but an inherent part of all creation. God, he said, is within each person. Jung also replaced the Trinity of the "Christian myth" with a quaternity: the Father, Holy Spirit, Christ, and Satan. ("Christ and Satan are both parts of God."[64])The Trinity was incomplete, he claimed, because it did not include evil—and *God must have a dark side*.

L'Engle also urges her readers to embrace God's dark side, but it is Jung who tells us what that dark side is: it's *Lucifer, Satan*.[65] He even denied that Satan was evil, calling him our "shadow," our insecure and incomplete nature. In order to be completely whole, a person must *"integrate the devil."*[66] According to Jung, it was a psychiatrist's obligation to help the patient incorporate Satan into their lives![67]

Jung, an evolutionist, believed God was a product of the unconscious and therefore had to evolve, just as man had. Like L'Engle, Jung had a difficult time accepting God, Yahweh, as portrayed in the Old Testament.

In Jung's view, Yahweh is the God of the Jews, but a God without consciousness. How is this to be proved? Because of his encounter with Job. Job sees through the injustice done to him. . . . Yahweh is amoral, jealous, irritable, good and evil, but He is not responsible for His actions, for He is too unconscious to be moral.[68]

According to Jung, the incarnation was necessary because of the evils God perpetrated against Job.

> Job stands morally higher than Yahweh. In this respect the creature has surpassed the creator. . . . Job's superiority cannot be shrugged off . . . Job is morally superior to him and therefore he has to catch up and become human himself . . . Yahweh must become man precisely because he has done man a wrong.[69]

In other words, according to the late Carl G. Jung, Christ did not come to save men from sin, He came to save Himself.

Meister Eckhart

On 3 March 1991 Madeleine L'Engle presented an arts and spirituality workshop on *The Four Paths of Meister Eckhart*. Meister Eckhart, a member of the Dominican Order, was a fourteenth century mystic who was declared a heretic. His writings influenced Adolf Hitler and were held largely responsible for planting the seeds for the National Socialist movement of Germany. Even the Nazis had a fondness for Eckhart's teachings and declared him to be a "member in good standing" of their party.[70] During the time of the Nazi regime, an essay appeared based upon Meister Eckhart's teachings, entitled *Germany's New Religion*, written by Professor Wilhelm Hauer, who professed to be a disciple of that mystic.

Today, there is a great interest in Eckhart's teaching among some Marxist theorists and Zen Buddhists. His writings are particularly popular among New Agers—including Matthew Fox and David Spangler—as well as some professing Christians. Psychologist and writer Richard Foster quotes the German mystic favorably in his books.

Eckhart was a stoic pantheist who taught "that there resides in every man a Divine, uncreated spark of the

Godhead, making possible both a union with God and a genuine knowledge of his nature. . . ." Not only did he believe in the divinity of man, but he also taught reincarnation to his assigned group of Dominican contemplative nuns.[71]

Eckhart's writings contained large strains of "theosophical speculation," which included cabalistic beliefs of reincarnation, the Oneness of all things, and religious purification. In fact, Eckhart entitled one of his works *Six Theosophic Points.*

A recent petition has been made to Pope John Paul II to absolve Eckhart of any charges of heresy and to declare his works to be "an authentic expression of Christian mysticism as trustworthy guides to Christian life according to the Gospel." According to Peter Hebblethwaite, a Vatican affairs writer from Oxford, there is every chance this will happen. The pope quoted Eckhart last September 28 in a seminar speech on Adrienne von Speyr, the Swiss mystical countess who inspired Father Hans Urs von Balthaser, leading theologian of this pontificate.[72]

New Age Dominican priest Matthew Fox calls Eckhart his favorite mystic and claims to actually communicate with this dead monk. Fox wrote a book called *Meditations with Meister Eckhart: A Centering Book* for all those daring to make the mystical, spiritual journey. This book is based on creation-centered spirituality and conjures up a series of early Catholic mystics including: Hildegard of Bingen, Julian of Norwich, Teresa of Avila, Nicholas of Cusa, Teilhard de Chardin, and Native Americans. Fox quotes Eckhart as saying there is a four-fold path to God, the last being something "deep" called "Breakthrough," where one begins to hear voices.

Meister Eckhart referred to true believing Christians as "ignorant people" who imagined that created things existed outside of God. In other words, he believed ALL creatures are in God, and God is in ALL. He celebrated the divine image, what is traditionally called "cosmic wisdom" or the "Cosmic Christ." He compared God to a stone and to a fly because at the level of the divine gift of "isness" (existence), they are equal.

This, then, was the man who was the subject of Madeleine L'Engle's lecture at the Cathedral of St. John the Divine.

Theosophical Society

Through her written endorsement of *Kything*, Madeleine L'Engle puts her stamp of approval on several occult groups, including the most influential founding organization of the New Age movement, the Theosophical Society.

According to occult authority Dr. J. Gordon Melton,

> No single organization or movement has contributed so many components to the New Age Movement as the Theosophical Society. Founded in New York City in 1875 by Russian occultist Madame Helena Petrovna Blavatsky, Henry Steel Olcott and William Quan Judge, the society passed the occult tradition to more than 100 separate organizations in North American and many more in Europe, though its formal membership was only in the tens of thousands.[73]

The theosophical philosophies include the inter-connectedness of all matter, a divine plan for the world, the Great White Brotherhood, and all the aspects of reincarnation and karma. The Great White Brotherhood is believed by theosophists to be a spiritual hierarchy, guiding the destiny of humanity.

Upon the deaths of Blavatsky, Olcott, and Judge, Annie Bessant (author of *Esoteric Christianity*) emerged as the Theosophical Society's international president. With a close associate, occultist Charles W. Leadbeater, they began a campaign to bring forth a world spiritual teacher for the global federation that was geared to dawn at the end of this century. Their first candidate was discarded, and the second, Jiddu Krishnamurti, resigned after seventeen years of grooming. Throughout this time, the Theosophical Society was consumed with the preparation for "his" coming.

The Arcane School, set up as the vehicle to usher "the Christ" into his position, was founded by Alice Bailey,

who channeled twenty books by a disembodied spirit
(demon) calling himself Djwhal Khul, or "the Tibetan."
The books are blueprints for the new world order. Lucifer Publishing Co. was created to publish Bailey's works,
but on 11 November 1924 the name was changed to
Lucis Trust, for obvious reasons.

The Arcane School became the international spiritual organization for their disciples, teaching the principles of Ageless Wisdom, or Ancient Wisdom. Lucis Trust
provides worldwide financial support for the Arcane
School, the Lucis Publishing companies, World Goodwill,
Triangles, Lucis Trust Libraries, and Lucis Publications.

The book *Kything*, fully endorsed by Madeleine
L'Engle (as shown in chapter 2), promotes both the umbrella organization Lucis Trust and the Triangles Program, complete with an address to write. Alice Bailey
initiated Triangles in 1937, an on-going program that
brings people together in groups of three who unite in
meditation daily, to set the medium in which to speak
the Great Invocation.

Invoking the World Christ

When repeated while visualizing, Bailey considered
the Great Invocation a critical vehicle to call forth the
world savior. After Krishnamurti resigned, "Bailey offered an alternative by predicting a reappearance of the
Christ, also identified as the Bodhisattva *Maitreya* in
the spiritual hierarchy."[74] The following Great Invocation is now used by New Agers throughout the world,
calling forth Maitraya.

From the point of Light within the Mind of God
Let Light stream forth into the minds of men.
Let Light descend on Earth.

From the Point of Love within the Heart of God
Let love stream forth into the hearts of men.
Let Christ return to earth.

From the center where the Will of God is known
Let purpose guide the little wills of men—
The purpose which the Masters know and serve.

From the center which we call the race of men
Let the Plan of Love and light work out.
And may it seal the door where evil dwells.
Let Light and Love and Power restore the Plan on Earth.

The Theosophical Publishing House was developed with centers in Adyar, India; Wheaton, Illinois; and London, England. Wheaton became the headquarters for the Theosophical Society in America. Quest, the Theosophical bookstore in Wheaton—which sells L'Engle's books—is located just a few miles down the road from Wheaton College, where a special section of the library has been dedicated to Madeleine L'Engle.

OOO

The "Mythical Bible"

"The Bible is not a moral book. It is not an ethical book. It is a magnificent story book. It doesn't give any answers, it just tells more stories"

—Madeleine L'Engle, interview in *The Door*,
December 1986 p. 25.

"All Scripture is God-breathed and is useful for teaching, rebuking, correcting and training in righteousnes . . . so that the man of God may be thoroughly equipped for every good work"

—II Tim. 3:16.

"Did God really say?" was the question Satan so cleverly used to deceive Eve in the Garden of Eden. He knows that without a solid trust in the inerrant Word of God, our foundation and hope for salvation crumbles. Perhaps that is why the denial of biblical authority is at the heart of all heresy. Madeleine L'Engle has chosen to deny the accuracy and authority of Scripture. Virtually every book she has written undermines this essential doctrine.

Is the Bible inerrant? Of course not, she implies sarcastically in *And It Was Good*: "I do not need to believe that it was divinely dictated by God in a long beard and white gown. . . . It is a great storybook written over a great many centuries by many people."[1] It is a book written by man. "Men. . . . the Bible was set down by lots of people over lots of years. Centuries."[2] While the Bible claims to be "God-breathed," L'Engle even goes so far as to compare the author of the Genesis flood account to fallen angels. "'Listen, it's a stupid story. Only the males have names. It's a chauvinist story. . . .' The nephilim, [fallen angels] Dennys went on, 'They're just like whoever wrote the silly ark story, seeing things only from their own point of view, using people.'"[3] Is this any way to speak of the "Holy men of God who spoke as they were moved by the Holy Ghost"? (II Pet. 1:21) How far can one go without crossing the line?

Scorning those that fall for the "trap of literalism," L'Engle seduces her readers into believing God is not capable of preserving His Word without error. (How is that for contradiction? Only a limitless God could accomplish such a miracle!) She further contends that the "limited literalism which demands that the Bible's poetry and story and drama and parable be taken as factual history is one of Satan's cleverest devices."[4]

Rejecting the divine inspiration of God, L'Engle espouses the New Age concept articulated by Joseph Campbell, Jean Houston, M. Scott Peck, and others that the Bible is a book of myth and symbol, containing truth, but not to be taken literally.[5] It's just simply one book of many myths and legends, which reveal an element of truth. "These marvelous mysteries could not be understood in the language of literalism, or inerrancy, and all such attempts to restrict the glory are deadly indeed."[6]

Webster defines myth as "a fable, an invented story, an imaginary person or thing." Proponents of New Age philosophies weave a web of deceit by calling myth truth and truth myth. Using this circular reasoning, they fool many Christians by claiming to believe that the Bible is true. But for them, fairy tales are true, and we all create our own reality. L'Engle explains, "Reality is something we participate in making, as co-creators with God. Making reality is part of our vocation, and one of the chief concerns of prayer. And it is an affirmation of interdependence."[7]

If reality is something that we make up, then there can be no absolute truth. In that case, truth would depend completely on each person's perception, and that perception can change from moment to moment. L'Engle asks, "Truth, for instance: we all want truth, that truth which Jesus promised would make us free. But where do we find it? How could it have happened that even in the church the story has been lost as a vehicle of truth?"[8] But story, or myth, is not truth.

So what is the purpose of the Scriptures, this collection of "myths and stories"? Madeleine L'Engle claims it is to reveal universal truths and to show the evolution of man's concept of God from the judgmental Old Testament God to the more loving "Abba" of the New Testament. And since man continues to evolve, L'Engle reasons, so should our myths. She says, "One of the most fascinating aspects of reading the Old Testament is to see the perception of God changing throughout the ages, so that the Abba to whom Jesus prayed is seen as different from the tribal god who helped Israel's kings destroy entire nations and peoples in order to give the land to the Israelites. (Are most wars over land boundaries?)"[9]

Joseph Campbell addressed this issue in *The Power of Myth.* "The old-time religion belongs to another age, another people, another set of human values, another universe. By going back you throw yourself out of sync with history."[10] L'Engle wholeheartedly agrees. Placing the Bible on the same plane as any religious book, she states, "The Bible . . . urges us to go beyond its pages, not to stop with what we have read."

By stripping the Bible of its inerrancy and relegating it to the realm of fairy tale, L'Engle feels free to alter God's Word to fit her personal theology. For example, she supports her belief in evolution by calling Adam and Eve "mythic ancestors" and denying the creation account of Scripture. Evolution is an essential element in occult and New Age philosophies, so their proponents display a great animosity to the biblical accounts of Creation and the Flood. L'Engle, an outspoken evolutionist, has devoted an entire novel, *Many Waters*, to destroying the character and story of Noah.

In *And It Was Good, Stone for a Pillow*, and *Sold into Egypt: Joseph's Journey into Human Being*, published as part of the Wheaton Literary Series, she blatantly rewrites the Old Testament, incorporating her own twisted view of the "paternalistic male chauvinist pig Old Testament god."[11] "But God, El,* the God of Joseph and the patriarchs, seems to be almost two separate gods, the tribal god . . . who still offends many people today and the God who was the maker of the universe."[12] "The righteous Lord of the Old Testament is an analogy of human righteousness as it was understood then."[13]

While mocking "this angry god, out to zotz us,"[14] L'Engle glorifies the idols of the Canaanites, falsely portraying them as kindlier, female goddesses. She contrasts these loving pagans to the Hebrews who wanted "to box God in." "The ancient Hebrews wanted to hide the Tabernacle in the Holy of Holies, so the ordinary people couldn't see it. Christians are just as bad."[15]

According to her books, all of the wives of Noah's sons and of the patriarchs, with the exception of Sarah, worshipped these idols. And while Joseph worshipped the God of his fathers, he didn't care enough to share his faith with his wife or children. Instead, he sent them to worship at the pagan Temple of On. "Asenath, his wife is beautiful and loving. Their sons are bright and full of laughter. Are they Egyptians, or are they Jews? They go to the great stone temple with their grandfather, the priest of On. They watch the rising and the setting of the sun and sing the hymns. Sometimes I hear them talk about their father's God as of a distant stranger."[16] Are

---

*L'Engle continually refers to God as "El." Though "El" does mean "God" in Hebrew, it is usually used as a prefix, as in "El-Shaddai," "Elohim," and "El-Bethel." However, the Canaanites also had a god called "El" who was lord over the other pagan deities. Who does Madeleine L'Engle mean when she refers to El? Is she speaking of the God of Abraham, Isaac, and Jacob, or one of the pagan deities from Canaan?

we to believe that Manasseh and Ephraim, who were to become fathers of two of the twelve tribes of Israel, had not been taught about the true God? If Joseph was indeed the man God portrays him to be, he would not have raised his children in Egyptian idolatry.

As the story continues, we realize that Asenath also wonders about Joseph's God but comes to the conclusion that "his god, too has limits. . . . Does he not care for all the rest of us, whether we live or die? This god my husband obeys does not hear the cry of anguish of the egyptian mother whose child is caught by the crocodile. Only his own people matter to him."[17]

L'Engle has Joseph going to his father-in-law, a pagan priest, for counsel. Joseph calls him "very wise" and marvels at the dreams that the sun god has given to this idolatrous man—dreams that even Joseph with his God-given gift of interpretation cannot understand. "I listen to the many stories of gods who live in the sun and in the sea, and in the moon, and also in strange beasts."[18] In L'Engle's book, Joseph listens and is awed by the holiness of this pagan priest.

L'Engle's desecration of God's Holy Word does not stop with the Old Testament. The Gospels give a detailed record of the death, burial, resurrection, and ascension of Jesus Christ. These accounts, however, do not jive with Madeleine L'Engle's personal theology, so in the name of "myth," they are conveniently thrown out. "What really happened has been lost in the mist of two thousand years. . . . So the Ascension is freed to move to the realm of myth."[19] Joseph Campbell says that very same thing in *The Power of Myth*.

But is Madeleine L'Engle really advocating that we create a new "myth," a new God, and rid ourselves of the just and righteous Lord of the Bible? That is precisely what she is doing. The following passage from her book, *Camilla*, makes this very plain.

> You know what we need is a new God . . . I mean, what we need is a God people like me, or David, or you, or our parents, could really believe in. I mean,

look at all the advances we've made scientifically since—oh, well, since Christ was born if you want to put a date on it. . . . But you take God. God hasn't changed any since Jesus took him out of a white nightgown and long whiskers. Along about when Christ was born, just a few years A.D., it was time someone should conceive a new God and then have the power to give his new understanding to the world. So what we need again now is a new God. The God most people are worshipping in churches and temples hasn't grown since Christ's time. He's deteriorated. . . . We need a God who's big enough for the atomic age.[20]

Joseph Campbell makes a similar bid for a new myth, a new God: "Each needs its own myth, all the way."[21] "The story that we have in the West, so far as it is based on the Bible, is based on a view of the universe that belongs to the first millennium B.C. It does not accord with our concept either of the universe or of the dignity of man. It belongs entirely somewhere else."[22]

To avoid this "trap of mythology," Christians need to become grounded in God's Word so they can discern between myth and truth. II Timothy 4:3-4 warns, "For the time will come when man will not put up with sound doctrine. Instead, to suit their own desires, they will gather around them a great number of teachers to say what their itching ears want to hear. They will turn their ears away from the truth and turn aside to myths." This is exactly what Madeleine does. Throughout her writings she changes the truth of God's Word into lying fables and myth. And upon the basis of a "mythical Bible," she redefines Christianity.

CHAPTER TEN

OOOOOOOOOOOOOOOOOOOOOOOOOOOOOOOOOOOOOOOOOOOOOO

Another Gospel

"But there were also false prophets among the people, just as there will be false teachers among you. They will secretly introduce destructive heresies, even denying the sovereign Lord who bought them, bringing swift destruction on themselves. Many will follow their shameful ways and will bring the way of truth into disrepute. In their greed these teachers will exploit you with stories they have made up. Their condemnation has long been hanging over them, and their destruction has not been sleeping."

—II Pet. 2:1-3.

Creation vs. Evolution

Madeleine L'Engle boasts publicly of her on-going study of science. According to her, scientists, or "modern mystics," are her theologians. Listeners might think she is referring to traditional physics, but what she and other New Agers are embracing is something called "particle physics," the study of "that which constructs time, space, and beyond; contains atoms, smaller particles, and vital life force." This is the same definition the *Donning Psychic Dictionary* gives for *cosmic consciousness*, the universal life force of the New Age. This theory claims that all matter is interconnected, and "aware of its function, it can be broken up and manipulated into different aspects for humanity's schooling and progression. Consequently, all matter is minutely connected and never detached from the whole; immeasurable, perfect, intelligent, whole . . ." Better defined, this is simply a rehashing of old pagan and esoteric beliefs.

The theory of evolution did not begin with Darwin, a Unitarian Universalist, but has been the root of pagan religions for centuries. The spiral of Evolution is fundamental to New Age philosophy, claiming that all life came from the same simple life form. Proponents believe we are still evolving up the spiral, and New Age/occultists are poised to take man on the final quantum leap: into godhood.

L'Engle defines evolution as man's "journey into human being." She claims we have only begun to be human, that "Jesus came to us as a truly human being, to show us how to be human, and we were so afraid of this humanness that we crucified it, thinking it could be killed."[1] She reiterated this at Calvin College, saying, "We are not yet human beings, we are only potentially human. I don't think we've gone much farther than those first humanoids who got up off all fours and were able to raise their forepaws and hold something and then chip rock and make tools and I can imagine them saying: 'We are man who can make tools. God has done it at last!' We probably have equally far to go in the journey towards being human."[2]

According to her, Christ became "fully God because he was incarnate more completely than anyone I have known."[3] In other words, Jesus became God because he had become fully human. And since Jesus was human, she explains, we can accomplish anything that he accomplished, including godhood. "But Jesus *was* us: isn't that the whole point? Jesus is us: and it's we who aren't us, and haven't been, not since Adam and Eve."[4]

L'Engle teaches the New Age heresy that we realize godhood by acquiring the "gifts" of the past: necromancy, mediumship, astral travel, ESP, witchcraft . . . and these are just a delightful few. Her books have even provided children with an example of the "Aquarian man" in her fictional character Charles Wallace, who is considered to be "new," having acquired ancient powers.[5] The "powers" are the key to unlocking the Universal Mind, the Higher Self. (It was Charles who was appropriately trained by Blajeny, the Hindu Satan.)

Militantly defending evolution, L'Engle puts down those who believe the Genesis creation account—comparing them to fools who still think the world is flat.* Perhaps the movement to destroy God's biblical creation account is a smoke screen for those who promote the theology of co-creation and of the occult theory of the interconnectedness of all things. According to occultists, men pull themselves up the spiral by their own spiritual bootstraps, so to speak. By denying God as creator, the special nature of man can also be denied, and nature moves up the spiral. Everything becomes interconnected. God becomes ALL.

But man, who was formed by God's own hands, *is* set apart from nature. Only to man did God give a spirit. Christ came to redeem only man and not nature.

Right and Wrong

"Thank God we do not have to make moral judgments . . ."—Madeleine L'Engle, *Sold Into Egypt, Joseph's Journey Into Human Being*, p. 113.

"Moralism belongs to the old law and the old covenant. Jesus Christ. . . . overturned the laws of moralism"—Madeleine L'Engle, *The Irrational Season*, p. 102.

"Let your light so shine before men, that they may see your good works, and glorify your Father which is in heaven. Think not that I am come to destroy the law, or the prophets: I am not come to destroy, but to fulfill"—Jesus, Matt. 5:16-18.

"Be ye holy; for I am holy"—I Pet. 1:16.

---

*For those who wish further information regarding scientific evidence for creation vs. evolution, Dr. Henry Morris and the Institute for Creation Research have produced excellent material, some of which is available at local Christian bookstores.

L'Engle embraces moral relativism, claiming God does not expect us to judge between good and evil, nor would we know how to do so. "A great deal of the time we do not know what is good and what is evil. We cannot tell our right hand from our left."[6] In this manner she attempts to eliminate a person's moral responsibility before God.

L'Engle continually exalts those acts that God forbids, promoting homosexuality, witchcraft, occult practices, Druids, and premarital sex. In fact, *House Like a Lotus* contains a graphic sex scene in which a sixteen-year-old loses her virginity—for children to read and enjoy.[7]

Sin

"Everyone who sins breaks the law: in fact, sin is lawlessness"—I John 3:4.

"Therefore, just as sin entered the world through one man, and death through sin, and in this way death came to all men, because all have sinned"—Rom. 5:12.

". . . for all have sinned and fall short of the glory of God"—Romans 3:23.

"And what is sin . . . sin is discourtesy"—Madeleine L'Engle, A Stone for a Pillow, p. 23.

In their quest for divinity, New Agers deny man's sinful nature. L'Engle attempts to accomplish this in two ways. First, she denies the sinlessness of Jesus Christ, thus pulling Him down to our level. Next, she redefines sin as a "lack of at-one-ment," a "discourtesy."[8] It is something easily overcome, and, of course, nothing that would separate us from God.

But what about original sin? Though L'Engle often refers to Adam and Eve, she denies their historical existence, parroting Joseph Campbell's view that the story of the Garden of Eden and the Fall simply represents a step in human evolution.

She describes the Fall as a mis-timed step toward knowledge.

> So they ate of the fruit of the tree of knowledge of good and evil, and the timing was all off; they weren't ready, and so the result was confusion. Ever since that first disastrous mistiming, we have grown in knowledge without being aware that we have not grown equally in spirit . . . Adam and Eve knew too much before they had grown enough to be ready for knowledge. . . . Adam and Eve were incapable of assimilating all that they suddenly knew. They saw that they were naked, and in their beautiful, created bodies they were embarrassed, not because they were cold, but because they suddenly knew more than they could possibly understand.[9]

To believe in man's sinful nature, she reasons, is to make excuses for our actions. "Sin, that unpopular word again. The worse things get, the more we try to rationalize and alibi. When we do wrong we try to fool ourselves (and others) that it is because our actions and reactions have been coded into our genetic pattern at the moment of conception."[10]

And so, L'Engle lightly dismisses man's sinful nature, the very reason for the Gospel.

The Atonement: A Sacrifice for Sin?

The very foundation of the salvation message of the Gospel of Jesus Christ, upon which every believer stands, is undermined in Madeleine L'Engle's words in *Stone for a Pillow*. "We are not meant to cringe before God, or to call on Jesus to come and save us from an angry and vengeful Father. . . ." "God is not like a judge sentencing a criminal. Yet far too often we view God as an angry judge who assumes that we are guilty unless we can placate divine ire and establish our innocence."

And in *The Irrational Season*:

> I doubt if it is given to the human being to understand completely the blessed passion and precious death . . . of our Lord Jesus Christ. I know that I do not understand. But I also know that it has

nothing to do with the angry, unforgiving God. . . . If
the basic definition of sin is lack of love . . . then an
inability to forgive is lack of love, and if God is
unable to forgive us then he is lacking in love, and
so he is not God. At least, he is not the God who
makes glad my heart.

God answers: "But God demonstrates His own love
for us in this: While we were still sinners, Christ died for
us. Since we have now been justified by His blood, how
much more shall we be saved from God's wrath through
Him!" (Rom. 5:8-9) "For this is my blood of the new
covenant, which is poured out for many for the forgive-
ness of sins" (Matt. 26:28).

Before the Fall, Adam and Eve enjoyed sweet communion with God. But when the serpent came, man
chose to disobey his wonderful Creator. Suddenly, the
communion was shattered. Sin separated them from God.
They were dying, doomed to face eternity with their
seducer.

But God, who is a holy and righteous judge, could not
ignore His holiness. Out of the abundance of His great
love, He had already devised a plan to pay the debt of
sin. He would provide a substitute, an atonement.

According to *Webster*, the word *atonement* means "rec-
onciliation of God and man through the death of Jesus
Christ; the reparation or payment of a debt." This definition is evident throughout all of Scripture. In the Old
Testament, God commanded that a lamb be sacrificed at
regular intervals as a substitutionary atonement for sins,
and each time the word atonement appears in Scripture
it is used in this context. These sacrifices were a picture
of the "Lamb of God who taketh away the sins of the
world" (John 1:29)—Jesus Christ. And though Christ
was yet to come, those who by faith obeyed God's command and brought their sacrifice were forgiven (Heb.
11).

Finally, "when the fullness of time was come (Eph.
1:10)," God Himself came down to earth to be our substitute: Jesus Christ, the eternal Son of God, Immanuel,
God incarnate.

However, Madeleine L'Engle does not choose to believe that we are fallen, sinful creatures who are "dead" in our "trespasses and sins" as the Scriptures tell us. She calls this a "forensic" or judgmental view of God. God cannot be angry, she reasons, for anger is sin, and then God would be a sinner. But if this rationale is true, how do we account for verses such as these? "Be angry and sin not" (Eph. 4:26). "God judgeth the righteous, and God is angry with the wicked every day" (Ps. 7:11). What about the hundreds of references in Scripture about God's wrath and judgment? And what do we do with the Righteous Judge of the book of Revelation?

As usual, when L'Engle encounters something in Scripture she doesn't like, she simply changes it. Calling a God who would allow His son to die a "bad-tempered father" and "cartoon forensic god," she mocks the heart of the Gospel, the substitutionary atonement for sin— the purpose and work of our Lord Jesus Christ.[11]

Cleverly, L'Engle redefines the atonement to mean at-one-ment, as New Age guru Shirley MacLaine does in her book, *Out on a Limb*. MacLaine says that atonement is "At-one-ment with the original creator or with the original creation."[12] The New Age definition of at-one-ment simply means to be "at one with God," which presents a monistic/pantheistic theology. It is also defined as being "in tune with God," or atunement.

A Course in Miracles expands this heresy. *A Course* is a New Age bible channeled by a demon, who calls himself "Jesus," through University of Columbia professor Helen Schucman.

> The crucifixion did not establish the atonement . . . many sincere Christians have misunderstood this . . . if the crucifixion is seen from an upside-down point of view, it does appear as if God permitted and even encouraged one of His Sons to suffer because he was good. This particularly unfortunate interpretation . . . has led many people to be bitterly afraid of God . . . I was not "punished" because you were bad . . . God does not believe in retribution.[13]

L'Engle mimics this demonology in *Stone for a Pillow*:

> A young friend said to me during Holy Week, "I cannot cope with the atonement."
>
> Neither can I, if the atonement is thought of forensically. In forensic terms, the atonement means that Jesus had to die for us in order to atone for all our awful sins, so that God could forgive us. In forensic terms, it means that God cannot forgive us unless Jesus is crucified and by this sacrifice atones for all our wrong doing.
>
> But that is not what the word means. . . . It means exactly what it says, at-one-ment. . . . There is nothing about crime and punishment in the makeup of that word. It simply means to be at one with God.[14]

Continuing this blasphemy, she adds:

> If the totally interdependent, interconnected world of physics is true, then this oneness affects the way we look at everything. It radically affects the way we look at the cross. Jesus on the cross was at-one with God, and with the infinite mind, in which Creation is held. The anguish on the cross has to do with this at-one-ment in a way which a forensic definition of atonement cannot even begin to comprehend.[15]

While redefining atonement, L'Engle continually reiterates her Hindu belief in the "God who is One, the God who is All."[16]

She further mocks God by proclaiming it is heresy to believe that Christ died to save us from our sins! In *The Irrational Season* (which is *definitely irrational*), she writes:

> One of my young married students has suffered all her life because she was taught in her Church that she was born so sinful that the only way the wrath of God the Father could be appeased enough for him to forgive all her horrible sinfulness was for God the Son to die in agony on the cross. Without

his suffering, the Father would remain angry forever with all his Creation.

Many of us have had at least part of that horror
thrust on us at one time or other in our childhood.
For many reasons I never went to Sunday School,
so I was spared having a lot of peculiar teaching to
unlearn. It's only lately that I've discovered that it
was no less a person than St. Anselm who saw the
atonement in terms of appeasement of an angry
God, from which follows immediately the heresy
that Jesus came to save us from God the Father.[17]

In an attempt to discredit those who teach and believe in biblical redemption, she deliberately misrepre-
sents them as sadists. "If eternal damnation is part of
our mindset, it is far too easy to wonder if part of the joy
of the saved in heaven is looking down on the tortures of
the damned."[18]

Is this L'Engle's picture of Jesus Christ? He also
taught that there was a place of eternal damnation. The
Bible makes it very clear that it was not an angry, hateful God who unfeelingly sent His Son to die for us. Jesus,
God incarnate, came as a precious gift of love. "This is
how God showed his love among us: He sent his one and
only Son into the world that we might live through him.
This is love: not that we loved God, but that he loved us
and sent his Son as an atoning sacrifice for our sins" (I
John 4:9-10). "But if anybody does sin, we have one who
speaks to the Father in our defense—Jesus Christ, the
Righteous One. He is the atoning sacrifice for our sins,
and not only for ours but for the sins of the whole world"
(1 John 2:1b-2).

The Last Judgment and the Second Coming

"I know a number of highly sensitive and intelligent
people in my own community who consider as a heresy
my faith that . . . he [God] will not rest until all of
creation, including Satan, is reconciled to him, until there
is no creature who cannot return his look of love with a

joyful response of love"—Madeleine L'Engle, *The Irrational Season*, p. 97.

"Then He will say to those on His left, 'Depart from
me, you who are cursed, into the eternal fire prepared for
the devil and his angels . . . Then they will go away to
eternal punishment, but the righteous to eternal life"—
Jesus, Matt. 25:41, 46.

"And I saw a great white throne, and Him that sat on
it, from whose face the earth and the heaven fled away;
and there was found no place for them. And I saw the
dead, small and great, stand before God: and the books
were opened: and another book was opened, which is the
book of life. . . . And whosoever was not found written in
the book of life was cast into the lake of fire"—Rev.
20:11-12, 15.

In order to embrace the New Age definitions for sin
and atonement, L'Engle must also redefine the Last
Judgment and the Second Coming.

In *Stone for a Pillow*, she writes: "The judgment of
God is the judgment of love, not of power plays or vindi-
cation or hate. The Second Coming is the redemption of
the entire cosmos, not just one small planet. . . . all will
be redeemed in God's fullness of time, all, not just the
small portion of the population who have been given the
grace to know and accept Christ."[19] In this, L'Engle has
clearly called God's Word a lie and Christ's death needless. Acts 4:12 (NIV) says: "Salvation is found in no one
else; for there is no other name under heaven given to
men by which we must be saved."

She teaches that salvation is found in ourselves, not
in someone else, including Jesus Christ. God's Word,
however, says the opposite. "For it is by grace you have
been saved, through faith—and this is not from your-
selves, it is the gift of God—not by works, so that no one
can boast" (Eph. 2:8-9; NIV). L'Engle's view of the Last
Judgment is as twisted as her view of atonement ("For
God's judgment is atonement, at-one-ment, making us
one with the Lord of Love").

Once again, her doctrine is strikingly similar to the

theology contained in *A Course in Miracles*. An interesting coincidence, in light of her constant protest that she knows little about the New Age movement. Note how the identical nature of the heresies, however, shows that her "theology" comes from the same source, the "father of all lies" John 8:44c, (NASB).

In *A Course in Miracles*, the New Age definition of the Last Judgment parallels L'Engle's. Here, the demon who calls himself "Jesus" contends that "judgment is not an attribute of God. . . . The Last Judgment is . . . a final healing rather than a meting out of punishment, however much you may think that punishment is deserved."[20] "Salvation is God's justice . . . God's judgment is His justice—a Judgment wholly lacking in condemnation; an evaluation based entirely on love."[21]

According to New Agers, there is no "day of judgment" when God will pour out his fury on those who have rejected him. L'Engle says:

> Confusing punishment with revenge has further confounded us into confusing judgment with vindictiveness. Far too many people fear the Last Judgment because they believe God is really going to zotz them for all their wrong-doings, tearing off the few Brownie points they've acquired and trampling them in the dust.
>
> Or, what is worse, they look forward to the Last Judgment because that is when God is really going to zotz all their enemies, and they, the saved, can rejoice in the torments of the damned in hell.[22]

But what does God say? Will Jesus actually return to earth some day as promised?

> For the Lord himself shall come down from heaven with a loud command, with the voice of the archangel and with the trumpet call of God, and the dead in Christ will rise first. After that, we who are still alive and are left will be caught up with them in the clouds to meet the Lord in the air. And so will we be with the Lord forever. (I Thess. 4:16-17)

Unfortunately, L'Engle once again rejects God's Word. If anyone is foolish enough to believe God's Word, she explains, then he has obviously fallen into the "trap of literalism." To emphasize her point, she tells a story about her son-in-law, Alan Jones, pastor of Grace Cathedral in San Francisco. Alan "was asked once by a pious woman if our feet would be wafted from the earth, at the time of the Second Coming, before Jesus's feet touched ground." With a sarcastic tone L'Engle retorts: "Ouch. That kind of literalism is not what it's about."[23]

So, what *is* it about? She's happy to explain. "The Coming of the Kingdom is creation coming to be what it was meant to be, the joy and glory of all creation working together with the Creator."[24] Near the end of that book, she continues, "When I think of the phrase the Coming of the Kingdom it means to me the restoration of community, the healing of brokenness which will enable us to rejoice once more in being one—not a solitary, isolated one, but whole, body, intellect, spirit at peace; mind, heart, intuition in collaboration."[25]

The Second Coming, or the Last Judgment (in New Age theology they are the same), is defined similarly in *A Course of Miracles* as "Christ restored as one identity, in which the Sons of God acknowledge that they are all one" and "the correction of mistakes, and the return of sanity."[26]

New Agers assert that the Second Coming is not the return of Christ to earth. L'Engle defines it as a time when everyone discovers that they are part of the Trinity. But doesn't "Trinity" mean three? It doesn't have to, L'Engle replies. "The Trinity is unity in diversity; the Trinity is our model for community."[27] And again, she asks, why should we limit God to his Word? "If he is indeed the maker of the galaxies, isn't three a small number for his persons? Aren't there probably dozens, if not millions?"[28]

What will L'Engle and other New Age followers do when they find out that they are not gods? This is the same question God asked the king of Tyre in Ezekiel 28:2 (NASB). "Thus says the Lord God, 'Because your heart is lifted up And you have said, I am a god, I sit in the seat of gods, In the heart of the seas; Yet you are a man and not God . . .'"

Heaven and Hell

L'Engle says:

"Some churches remain stuck in the old literal representations of heaven and hell. . . . They are still good metaphors, but no longer to be taken literally" (*Sold Into Egypt: Joseph's Journey Into Human Being*, p. 140; part of the Wheaton Literary Series).

"I don't understand why the idea of emptying hell upsets some people so. To be upset about it is to think forensically" (*Stone for a Pillow*, p. 179).

God says:

"Fear him who, after the killing of the body, has power to throw you into hell. Yes, I tell you, fear him" (Luke 12:5b; NIV).

"Then I saw a new heaven and a new earth: for the first heaven and the first earth were passed away" (Rev. 21:1).

Because she does not believe in eternal damnation for those who reject Christ as Savior, L'Engle can say with confidence, "For me Gandhi is a Christ figure. I'll be perfectly happy to go wherever he goes. If you want to call that hell, that's your problem."[29]

Throughout her writings, she focuses on getting her readers to question God's Word by putting guilt trips on them. According to her, if we believe in heaven and hell, then we must also believe "the joy of the saved in heaven is looking down on the tortures of the damned." Who, but the "father of all lies," a "murderer from the beginning" (John 8:44; NIV), Satan himself, would want us to believe that there will be no eternal damnation as a consequence for rejecting the gospel of Christ?

L'Engle rebukes those who believe that "heaven is for

Christians only," calling it a "judgmental (if not forensic) attitude, not "true to the love of God."[30]

Where then, or what is, heaven? "Wherever God is, heaven is, and if I don't have glimpses of it here and now, I'm not going to know it anywhere else," says L'Engle. "The Coming of the Kingdom" is "the restoration of community."[31] L'Engle is espousing the New Age concept that "heaven" (utopia) will be here on earth when all live together and dwell in harmony, peace, and wholeness— "unity in diversity"—eating together at a "heavenly banquet."[32]

L'Engle further suggests that a "belief in [a literal] hell is a lack of faith because it is to attribute more power to Satan than to God."[33] "To be in a state of unforgiveness is to know hell at least in some small way. I know, because I've been there."[34] But she makes it very clear that we can get out of hell ourselves, she asserts that "it's not easy to get out of hell, but it can be done."[35]

How is this feat accomplished? "When we come to ourselves and turn to the source of all love."[36] This may not sound too unreasonable until the reader realizes L'Engle defines the "source" as the God who is within all creation: trees, rocks, animals, and humanity. According to L'Engle's theology, since we are "co-creators" with God, we can save ourselves. All we need to do is recognize our own divinity.

New Age teacher, Elizabeth Clare Prophet, writes in her book, *The Lost Teachings of Jesus 2*, "We have got to learn that we are acting creatively as God acts creatively, that we are co-creators with him of our destiny and that by purifying our thoughts—the offspring of our minds— we will be siring a true and noble lineage made in the image of our Christ."[37]

Echoing this statement, L'Engle asserts, "God is constantly creating in us, through us, with us, and to co-create with God is our human calling. It is the calling for all of us."[38]

In *And It Was Good*, L'Engle provides a handbook on co-creating. She acquaints the reader with the Hindu concept that God is within everyone or, more precisely, that everyone is God. She describes the Hindu greeting of *Namaste*, "I salute the God within you," and calls it beautiful.[39]

Satan

"Fallen angel or no, Satan was still God's son, and at that point was still speaking with his Creator. I wonder if he is still willing to do that, or if he has so separated himself from at-one-ment that he and his cohorts can no longer bear to be in the Presence?"—Madeleine L'Engle, *A Stone for a Pillow*, p. 80.

"No matter how many eons it takes, he [God] will not rest until all of creation, including Satan, is reconciled to him, until there is no creature who cannot return his look of love with a joyful response of love"—Madeleine L'Engle, *The Irrational Season*, p. 97.

"For to which of the angels did God ever say, 'You are my Son; today I have become your Father' Or again, 'I will be his Father, and he will be my Son'? And again, when God brings His firstborn into the world, he says, 'Let all God's angels worship him'"—Heb. 1:5-6 (NIV).

"Then He will say to those on his left, 'Depart from me, you who are cursed, into the eternal fire prepared for the devil and his angels"—Jesus, Matt. 25:41 (NIV).

New Age gurus David Spangler and Barbara Marx Hubbard teach that Satan is God's Son, that Lucifer is actually the same force as Christ. This is represented by the "yin and the yang" of eastern religions, or the dark and light sides of the Divine, as L'Engle describes it. By claiming that Satan is God's son, she has made him equal to the second person in the Trinity, our Lord and Savior Jesus Christ. In fact, she says all angels are God.[40] To equate Jesus with the defiler of the world is the ultimate in heresy!

L'Engle also teaches that the mark of the Beast will

be redeemed. Revelation 13:18 (NIV) identifies this mark:
". . . If anyone has insight, let him calculate the number
of the beast, for it is man's number. His number is 666."
In response to this passage, L'Engle assures us that "the
beast is often assumed to be Satan. . . . But even numbers, when abused, can be redeemed, and ultimately 666
will return to God."[41]

Do not be deceived by these seductive lies. This is the
spirit of Antichrist! We are made in God's image, not
Satan's. And those who take upon themselves the mark
of Anti-christ have *forever* alienated themselves from
God. God is not mocked, and the reception that is planned
for those who bear the Beast's mark is far different from
that painted by L'Engle!

> If anyone worships the beast and his image and
> receives his mark on the forehead or on the hand,
> he, too, will drink of the wine of God's fury, which
> has been poured full strength into the cup of his
> wrath. He will be tormented with burning sulfur
> in the presence of the holy angels and of the Lamb,
> and the smoke of their torment rises forever and
> ever. There is no rest day or night for those who
> worship the beast and his image, or for anyone
> who receives the mark of his name. (Rev. 14:9b-11;
> NIV)

Reincarnation

"Perhaps the question of reincarnation has come to
the forefront of people's thinking about life and death
because the Church has held back. . . . stuck in the old
literal representations of heaven and hell. . . . There is
nothing inconsistent with Christianity in such consider-
ations . . ."—Madeleine L'Engle, *Sold Into Egypt*: *Joseph's
Journey Into Human Being*, p. 140-141.

"Just as man is destined to die once and after that to
face judgment, so Christ was sacrificed once to take away
the sins of many people; and he will appear a second
time, not to bear sin, but to bring salvation to those who
are waiting for him"—Heb. 9:27-28 (NIV).

Madeleine L'Engle is reluctant to publicly proclaim a belief in reincarnation. Yet she subtly weaves this doctrine throughout her writings. For example, she claims that Judas and Nero will both learn, in time, to receive Christ.

> It may take more years than we can count before Nero—for instance—has learned enough love to be able to look with joy into the loving eyes of a Christ who enfleshed himself for a time on earth as a Jew, but Nero's punishments, no matter how terrible they may be, are lessons in love, and that love is greater than all his sick hate.[42]

And again:

> He [God] will not rest until Judas has turned to him, until Satan has turned to him, until the dark has turned to him; until we can all, all of us without exception, freely return his look of love in our own eyes and hearts. And then, healed, whole, complete but not finished, we will know the joy of being co-creators with the one to whom we call.[43]

Judas and Nero are both dead. Where and when are they to learn all of these marvelous lessons? In *Camilla* L'Engle gives us a hint.

> So what I figured out was this: nobody ever gets a chance to finish on this Earth. And even if there's a heaven nobody's good enough at the end of life on this earth to be ready to go to heaven. . . . So I figured that when we die, maybe we go to another planet, the next planet in the scale. . . . And then when we'd finished on that planet we'd go on to another planet and develop even more, and so on and on and on, for hundreds and thousands or maybe even millions of planets, learning and growing all the time, until at last we'd be ready for heaven.[44]

There is no doubt that in her books, Madeleine L'Engle teaches the concept of reincarnation.

Conclusion

God warned that we should not trust everyone who comes in His name. II John 1:11 (NIV) commands: "If anyone comes to you and does not bring this teaching, do not take him into your house or welcome him. Anyone who welcomes him shares in his wicked work."

OO

Another Christk

Another Christ

"It is always God the Son I find most difficult: the man Jesus of Nazareth, the dead Jew, is my stumbling block"

—Madeleine L'Engle, *The Irrational Season*, p. 168.

"'But what about you,' he asked. 'Who do you say I am?' Simon Peter answered, 'You are the Christ, the Son of the Living God.' Jesus replied, 'Blessed are you, Simon son of Jonah, for this was not revealed to you by man, but by my Father in heaven'"

—Matt. 16:15-17 (NIV).

"Who is Jesus Christ?" is a good question to ask when examining Madeleine L'Engle's books. The image she paints is in direct contrast to the Christ of the New Testament. Who is Jesus? He is the "virgin born Son of God," "totally human" and "totally God," L'Engle explains. Appearing to be doctrinally sound on the surface, a closer look at her writings reveals that she has redefined most aspects of Christ's birth, life, nature, death, and resurrection.

The Virgin Birth

L'Engle gives lip service to the biblical doctrine of the divinely engineered virgin birth of Christ, calling it a "Glorious Impossible," but holds a very different concept of what constitutes a "virgin birth." Joseph Campbell, in

The Power of Myth,[1] claims, "The Messiah as the son of God is not actually God's son," and compares the biblical account of the virgin birth to the rape of Leda by Zeus (represented by a swan).

In her poem, "Bearer of Love," L'Engle develops this comparison. The first two stanzas graphically describe Leda's "wild" rape and Zeus's "lust deepened by the terror on her face." The poem suddenly focuses on Mary, who "acquiesced" when approached by the angel Gabriel, whose "wings were wilder than the swan [Zeus]." Gabriel gave her the "lily's sword thrust and was gone." L'Engle explains that the old gods "fall in consternation at the fierce coming of the wild wind's thrust entering Mary in pure penetration."[2] She refers to Mary's seducer as both God and Gabriel interchangeably. The reason for this may be her belief that angels are God. "They [angels] are God come to tell us something. . . . To be visited by an angel is to be visited by God."[3]

The Childhood of Christ

The Bible reveals little about the childhood of Christ, but L'Engle is quick to fill in the gap, starting with *Dance in the Desert,* her version of the holy family's flight into Egypt. The story, full of symbolism, begins with the family seeking to join a caravan. The many dangers of the desert—eagles who steal children, lions, poisonous snakes, wild jackasses, unicorns who pierce travelers through with their horns, and dragons, all graphically illustrated—make traveling alone impossible.

Finally, a caravan allows the family to come along, and soon the pleasant toddler (Jesus) has won their hearts. Then came that special evening, after the fire was lit, when the animals came to "dance" with the child. First came a lion, then mice, wild jackasses, eagles, an adder, ostriches, a unicorn, a bleeding pelican, and dragons.

The visit of the snake is almost sensual in its description: "The snake moved around the child's leg in sinuous swirls of affection, its undulating movements shimmering along the delicate length of its body. The child stood

very still, looking down, smiling, pleased and unafraid."
Does this child sound like Christ or the Antichrist? Christ
came to crush the serpent's head.

As the unicorn entered the story, it became evident
that he was Lord of the desert. Because of his exalted
position, his visit is unique. Approaching the fire, he
"bowed his horned head . . . until it touched the sand
before the child in a gesture of loving reverence. Then he
walked past the child to the young mother, lay down
quietly beside her, and put his head in her lap." (The
unicorn is the occult/New Age symbol of the androgynous
Supreme Deity, the horn representing the male attached
to a female body—the yin and the yang of deification.)

When the unicorn departs, the other animals join
together in a great circular dance around the child. A
double-page spread is devoted to illustrate the final hom-
age. The red glow of the fire, the smiling child standing
in front, arms outstretched, and the horrible creatures of
the desert parading about the circle, form a shocking
picture reminiscent of a medieval illustration of hell.
Sometime during the final dance, the child returns to his
mother's lap and falls asleep, arms outstretched as though
embracing the beasts.

The Sphinx at Dawn continues the saga of Christ's
early life, describing his sojourn in Egypt. Jesus is identified by the Hebrew name "Yehoshuah," "Yos" for short.
In these stories he is described as "a good boy" but "head-
strong," once again undermining his sinless nature. Here,
the owls, camels, unicorns, and spirits of the dead under-
take his education, teaching Jesus the fine occult arts of
ESP and trance-like meditation. This mystical child is
already raising the dead and performing miracles, though,
according to the story, "Yos" has no idea that he is God
Incarnate. In this way, L'Engle portrays Jesus Christ as
a mystic. It's no coincidence that New Ager Matthew Fox
makes the same comparison in his book, *The Coming of
the Cosmic Christ.* He includes a chapter titled, "The
Historical Jesus as Mystic and Teacher of Mysticism."
Just before the return trip to Israel, the boy encounters
a very old man who directs him to visit the Egyptian

Sphinx to be tested. If any of the child's answers are incorrect, the Sphinx will eat the boy. That's no problem, however, because "Yos" shares the cannibalistic belief that the soul of whoever is eaten becomes a part of the devourer.

"Have you really eaten many men, Sphinx?"

"Many."

"Then you are many men, are you not? And if I cannot answer your riddles and you eat me, then you will be me, too."

"You will learn, child," the Sphinx said, "that we all live by eating of each other. If you eat only my words, you are a part of me."

The boy laughed up at the broken stone face.[4]

The riddles continue, but with the help of a camel who kythes with him, Christ answers them successfully. The child embraces the Sphinx who tells him, "We have shared each other's words, little son, and we are part of one another now. Wherever you go from now on you will always take with you some of my wisdom and some of my indignation and some of my pain." Isn't it strange that L'Engle's Christ was empowered with the wisdom of pagan idols? Hers is another Christ, not the Holy Savior of the Bible.

The Sinless Nature of Jesus Christ

"For he hath made him to be sin for us, who knew no sin; that we might be made the righteousness of God in him"—II Cor. 5:21.

"When I am informed that Jesus of Nazareth was exactly like us except sinless, I block. If he was sinless he wasn't exactly like us. That makes no sense . . . I want Jesus to be like us because he is God's show and tell, and too much dogma obscures rather than reveals the likeness"—Madeleine L'Engle, *A Stone for a Pillow*, p. 176.

Jesus Christ, though wholly man, was also wholly God. He was God manifested in the flesh and therefore was sinless. And because of this sinless nature, He was able to take upon Himself our punishment, to become sin for us. This is absolutely vital to the doctrine of salvation.

Instead, Madeleine L'Engle has chosen to deny and redefine the sinlessness of Christ. She subscribes to the beliefs of her good friend, M. Scott Peck, who admits:

> I am weak on traditional Christian redemption theology—which holds that Jesus is the spotless, sinless lamb that was sacrificed for us, and redeemed us. . . . There's a real question about whether or not Jesus was sinless, because Christian doctrine also hold that while he was fully divine he was also fully human, and I don't see how you can be wholly human and be sinless. Secondly, I worry about theology that says that because this or that was done, that we've been saved.[5]

Webster's definition of sin is "a transgression against divine or moral law." L'Engle redefines sin as not staying close to some cosmic source. She deceives Christians by concurring with Christ's perfect nature, yet accusing him of sin. "Jesus was sinless not because he didn't do wrong things: he broke the law, picking corn, for instance, on the Sabbath. He was sinless because he was never for a moment separated from the Source."[6] L'Engle ignores Christ's response to these charges. When rebuked, Jesus claimed that He had not broken the law, because "the Son of man is Lord of the Sabbath" (Matt. 12:8; NIV).

The Unique Divinity of Jesus Christ

New Agers like to separate Jesus of Nazareth from Christ. In his book, *The Coming of the Cosmic Christ*, Matthew Fox describes this cosmic Christ as "the Word" invading the universe and deifying all humanity and all creation. He says that Jesus was the embodiment of the cosmic Christ (but certainly not the *only* Christ), enabling us to rediscover our own divinity.

Madeleine L'Engle mirrors this New Age concept, saying, "My theology about Jesus of Nazareth and Jesus the risen Christ is always wobbly . . ."[7] We concur. L'Engle also distinguishes between Jesus and Christ, claiming that Jesus is "the man who housed the second person of the Trinity."[8] "Jesus of Nazareth lived for a brief life span, but Christ always was, is, and will be . . ."[9] How unfortunate she does not recognize Jesus as the Eternal Word of God.

And what was the purpose of Christ's coming? "Part of the meaning of the incarnation is that Jesus enChristed everything, giving it again the sacredness it had when the Word first spoke all of creation into being."[10] "Jesus came to us as a truly human being, to show us how to be human. . . ."[11] She changes God's call from "Be thou holy" to "Be thou human." In *Sold Into Egypt*, L'Engle says, "God does not ask us to be perfect; God asks us to be human."[12]

Pantheism is the Eastern belief adopted by the New Age movement that "God is all and all is God." Thus, God and his creation are not different in substance, but one. L'Engle constantly refers to God as the "God who is One, God who is All."[13] She urges us to "shed our idea of God as being someone Out There, separate from all that has been made, and begin instead to think of God as within all Creation, every galaxy, every quantum, every human being . . ."[14] "If I cannot see Christ in the maimed, in those possessed by devils, I cannot see Christ in the whole and holy."[15]

L'Engle relates a story about a pastor who had seen Hitler in World War II. "When it was all over, when Hitler's megalomaniac kingdom had fallen, and the world was trying to put itself back together and return to everyday living, it was remembered that he had seen Hitler. Someone asked him curiously, 'What did Hitler look like?' He replied quietly, 'Like Jesus Christ.' And that is what it is like to be pure in heart and to see God."[16]

Throughout her books, L'Engle repeatedly states that Jesus was divine, but then she believes that everyone is

divine, that we have been "enChristed" and "ingodded,"
and "are part of the trinity."[17] She says, "We are not
called to be Christians; we are called Christs. I find this
both challenging and freeing."[18]

Removing the uniqueness from Jesus Christ's divine
nature, L'Engle places Him on the same level as great
artists and other religious leaders. In *A Wrinkle in Time*,
the "angels" compare Jesus to Leonardo da Vinci,
Michelangelo, Shakespeare, Bach, Pasteur, Madame
Curie, Einstein, Schweitzer, Gandhi, and Buddha.[19] At
times when she needs encouragement, she says, "The
Buddha is a better Christ figure for me than the crucifix."[20] When walking home from the Cathedral of St.
John the Divine, L'Engle passes a statue of the Buddhist
saint, St. Shinran Shunin. Each night she prays, "'Good
night, Saint Shinran. Forgive us and help us,' and for
me, at that moment, Saint Shinran is one of God's angels."[21]

She further asserts that Jesus never claimed to be
the same as God the Father! "Worshipping Satan is more
like worshipping ourselves than anything else, and Jesus
never confused himself with the Father."[22] What is she
saying? If Jesus claimed to be God, would He be guilty of
Satan-worship? NO! Jesus, the sinless, only begotten of
the Father did indeed claim to be wholly God. He repeatedly asserted that "I and my Father are one" (John 10:30).

The Betrayal of Christ

"Then Satan entered Judas, called Iscariot, one of the
Twelve. And Judas went to the chief priests and the
officers of the temple guard and discussed with them
how he might betray Jesus. They were delighted and
agreed to give him money. He consented, and watched
for an opportunity to hand Jesus over to them when no
crowd was present"—Luke 22:3-6 (NIV).

"Judas is probably the most ambiguous character in
all of Scripture. Was he the most terrible villain in all of
history, betraying his master, conspiring with the high

priests to kill him? Or was he trying to force Jesus' hand,
to make him declare himself the Messiah, so that at last
the Jews would be free of the Roman yoke?"—Madeleine
L'Engle, *Glorious Impossible*, p. 31.

L'Engle once again rewrites Scripture. Was Judas
simply a friend, trying to help Jesus claim his throne?
Or was he "the son of perdition" as Jesus himself
identified him in John 17:12? L'Engle claims, "We shall
never know the real reason why Judas went to the chief
priests and said, 'What will you give me if I deliver
him to you?' . . . Was it for money? . . . . That does not
ring true . . . Was Judas frightened?"[23]

L'Engle continues on and on for literally pages elicit-
ing sympathy for Judas. "How strange and fearful it
must have been for Judas after he went to the priests
and promised them that he would betray Jesus. Did he
question himself as to whether or not he was doing the
right thing? Was he doing it for Jesus? Was he?"[24]

Why in the world would a Christian want to defend
Judas? L'Engle's attempt to paint him as a poor victim of
circumstance is reminiscent of the musical *Jesus Christ,
Superstar*. What makes it especially tragic is that her
book, *Glorious Impossible*, targets many young children
who have little exposure to the Bible.

The Death of Christ

"I am the good shepherd: the good shepherd lays
down his life for the sheep. . . . The reason my Father
loves me is that I lay down my life—only to take it up
again. No one takes it from me, but I lay it down on my
own accord. I have authority to lay it down and authority
to take it up again"—John 10:11, 17-18a,b (NIV).

"If he [Jesus] is truly one of us, wholly man as well as
wholly God, then his death is inevitable. All men must
die. All created matter ultimately comes to an end"—
Madeleine L'Engle, *The Irrational Season*, p. 88.

L'Engle flatly denies the true purpose of Jesus Christ's coming. Instead, she belittles his death, claiming it was merely part of the human experience. She does not believe that this sinless Jesus, the embodiment of the Godhead, became sin for us. For this perfect Son of God to be crushed under the weight of the evil of the world for all time, is unfathomable. Yet, in her unbelief, she is blinded to the message of the Cross. "I have long felt that the sacrifice of the mystery of the Word made flesh was a far greater sacrifice than the crucifixion. That was bad, yes. Terrible, yes. But it was three hours on the cross, three hours. . . . there are worse deaths."[25]

Because she denies the truth of God's Word, L'Engle sees the Cross as a symbol of failure, the failure of Jesus' mission here on earth to make us "more human." But the Bible very clearly shows that Christ's death, the purpose of the incarnation, was a victory. With his cry "It is finished," Jesus Christ secured salvation, conquered sin and death, and crushed the head of Satan.

The Resurrection and Ascension

"Jesus of Nazareth . . . was handed over to you by God's set purpose and foreknowledge; and you, with the help of wicked men, put him to death by nailing him to the cross. But God raised him from the dead, freeing him from the agony of death, because it was impossible for death to keep its hold on him"—Acts 2:22-24 (NIV).

"I believe in the resurrection of Jesus of Nazareth as Jesus the Christ. . . . not the literal resurrection of this tired body"—Madeleine L'Engle, *The Irrational Season*, p. 108-109.

"After a time, he ascended, whatever that means . . . Whatever really happened has been lost in the mists of two thousand years. . . . so the ascension is free to move into the realm of myth"—Madeleine L'Engle, *The Irrational Season*, p. 113-114.

Madeleine L'Engle does not believe that Jesus and Christ are the same. She calls Jesus a "dead Jew" who "lived a short life span," merely "housing" the Christ. This New Age doctrine is the basis for her denial of the bodily resurrection of Jesus Christ, as well as the future resurrection of mankind. She believes Jesus of Nazareth is still dead, but that the "Christ" he had housed was resurrected and is alive today, "engodding" all of creation. God, however, makes it perfectly clear that Jesus is the Christ, that He is the eternal Word who spoke the earth into existence. Jesus merely took on human form at the incarnation; He has always existed. After His resurrection, He made it clear that He was Jesus, in the flesh, not some mystical, cosmic source. And it is Jesus of Nazareth who now sits at the right hand of God.

This doctrine, which L'Engle repeatedly denies, is the foundation of our hope for eternity. "And if Christ has not been raised, your faith is futile; you are still in your sins. Then those also who have fallen asleep in Christ are lost. If only for this life we have hope in Christ, we are to be pitied more than all men" (I Cor. 15: 17-19).

Conclusion

Madeleine L'Engle may say "I accept Jesus as my Savior," but, the Jesus she preaches is not the one revealed in Scripture. She illustrates this with the following story:

> Two young women who run a Christian bookstore in the Midwest wrote me that they were concerned as to whether or not I accept Christ as my personal Savior. Even when I assured them that I do, they were not at all convinced that I was one of them. And perhaps the Christ I accept, by the grace of the Holy Spirit, is different from the Christ they want me to accept . . . I accept Christ as my personal Savior . . . Christ within me and within all of Creation . . .[26]

She does indeed have another Christ.

Notes

Introduction

1. Madeleine L'Engle, *The Irrational Season* (New York: The Seabury Press, 1979), 156.

2. Madeleine L'Engle, letter to the editor, *Today's Christian Woman*, (July/August, 1990).

3. 1992 Catalogue, *Omega: New Age Institute for Holistic Studies*.

Chapter 1: Fantasy? Or Occult 101

1. Madeleine L'Engle, *And It Was Good: Reflections on Beginnings* (Wheaton, Ill.: Harold Shaw Publishers, 1983), 21.

2. Madeleine L'Engle, *A Wind in the Door* (New York: Farrar, Straus and Giroux, 1968), 96.

3. Gerina Dunwich, *The Concise Lexicon of the Occult* (New York: Carol Publishing Group, 1990), 34, 174.

4. L'Engle, *And It Was Good*, 21.

5. Marilyn Ferguson, *The Aquarian Conspiracy* (Boston: Houghton Mifflin Co., 1980), 24.

6. Madeleine L'Engle, "Star-Gazer" (video) (New York: Ishtar Films, 1989).

7. Madeleine L'Engle, *A Wrinkle In Time* (New York: Farrar, Straus and Cudahy, 1962), 78.

8. Madeleine L'Engle, *Walking on Water: Reflections on Faith and Art* (Wheaton, Ill.: Harold Shaw Publishers, 1980), 85.

9. Ibid., 88.

10. Ibid., 86.

11. Ibid.

12. L'Engle, *And It Was Good*, 143.

13. Madeleine L'Engle, *Trailing Clouds of Glory: Spiritual Values in Children's Books* (Philadelphia: Westminster Press, 1985), 62-63.

14. Ibid.

15. Lind Goodman, *Star Signs* (New York: St. Martin's Press, 1965).

16. Anton Szandor LaVey, *The Satanic Bible* (New York: Avon Books, 1969), 51.

17. Madeleine L'Engle, *Sold Into Egypt: Joseph's Journey Into Human Being* (Wheaton, Ill.: Harold Shaw Publishers, 1989), 208.

18. Joseph Campbell with Bill Moyers, *The Power of Myth* (New York: Anchor Books, Doubleday, 1988), 25, 63.

19. Philip Yancey, ed., *Reality and the Vision* (Dallas: Word Publishing, 1990), 113.

20. G. J. Senick, ed., *Encyclopedia of Children's Literature Review* (Detroit: Gale Research Co., 1988), 139.

21. Madeleine L'Engle, "The Plausible Impossible" speech given at Wheaton College in Wheaton, Ill., 30 March 1990.

22. G.J. Senick, ed., *Encyclopedia of Children's Literature Review*, 139.

23. Madeleine L'Engle, *A Stone for a Pillow* (Wheaton, Ill.: Harold Shaw Publishers, 1984), 182-183.

24. *The Holy Bible*, New International Version.

25. Madeleine L'Engle, *The Irrational Season* (New York: The Seabury Press, 1979), 156.

26. Madeleine L'Engle, "Shake the Universe," *Ms. Magazine* (July/August, 1987): 184.

27. L'Engle, *A Wind in the Door*, 96.

28. Ibid., 114

29. P.M.H. Atwater, *The Magical Language of Runes* (Santa Fe, NM: Bear & Company, 1986), 28.

30. Madeleine L'Engle, *A Swiftly Tilting Planet* (New York: Farrar, Straus and Giroux, 1978).

31. Scott Cunningham, *The Truth About Witchcraft Today* (St. Paul, Minn.: Llewellyn Publications, 1988), 169.

32. L'Engle, *A Swiftly Tilting Planet*, 122.

Chapter 2: Occult 102

1. Glenn E. Estes, ed., *American Writers for Children Since 1900: Fiction* (Detroit: Gale Research Co., 1986), s.v. "Madeleine L'Engle."

2. *Something About the Author*, 27 (Detroit: Gale Research Co., 1982), 131-140.

3. June G. Bletzer, Ph.D., *The Donning International Encyclopedic Psychic Dictionary* (West Chester, Penn.: Schiffer Publishing, Ltd., 1986), s.v. "levitation."

4. Madeleine L'Engle, *Walking on Water: Reflections on Faith and Art* (Wheaton Ill.: Harold Shaw Publishers, 1980), 102.

5. Madeleine L'Engle, "Star-Gazer" (video) (New York: Ishtar Films, 1989).

6. Madeleine L'Engle, *And It Was Good: Reflections on Beginnings* (Wheaton, Ill.: Harold Shaw Publishers, 1980), 135.

7. Madeleine L'Engle, *The Summer of the Great-Grandmother* (New York: Farrar, Straus and Giroux, 1980), 96.

8. Ibid., 101.

9. Ibid.

10. Ibid.

11. Ibid., 103.

12. Kenneth Kelzer, *The Sun and the Shadow* (A.R.E. Press, 1987).

13. L'Engle, "Star-Gazer" (video).

14. L'Engle, *Walking on Water*, 194.

15. L'Engle, *And It Was Good*, 125.

16. Ibid., 9.

17. Ibid., 11.

18. Ibid., 86.

19. Ibid., 19.

Chapter 3: Jesus Christ: A Druid?

1. D.J. Conway, *Celtic Magic* (St. Paul, Minn.: Llewellyn Press, 1990), 83.

2. Madeleine L'Engle, "An Evening with Madeleine L'Engle: Readings and Dialogue," lecture given at Bethany Lutheran Church in Englewood, Colo. on 14 October 1989.

3. Dudley Wright, *Druidism: The Ancient Faith of Britain* (Yorkshire, Great Britain: EP Publishing, Ltd., 1974), 60.

4. Anne Ross and Don Robins, *The Life and Death of a Druid Prince* (New York: Summit Books, 1989), 53.

5. Ibid., 72.

6. Madeleine L'Engle, *An Acceptable Time* (New York: Farrar, Straus and Giroux, 1989), 132-133.

7. Ross and Robins, *Druid Prince*, 132.

8. L'Engle, *An Acceptable Time*, 162.

9. Sophie Moore, "The Gnosis Interview: Gwenc'hlan Le Scouezec," *Gnosis*, 6 (Winter 1988): 20.

10. Lewis Spence, *The History and Origins of Druidism* (New York: Samuel Webster, Inc., 1949), 104.

11. Stuart Piggott, *The Druids* (New York: Frederick A. Praeger, 1968), 110-112.

12. Spence, *The History and Origins of Druidism*, 89.

13. Ross and Robins, *Druid Prince*, 87.

14. Ibid., 134.

15. Ibid., 26.

16. Ibid., 162.

17. Ibid., 301, 303.

18. Madeleine L'Engle, *Walking on Water: Reflections on Faith and Art* (Wheaton Ill.:Harold Shaw Publishers, 1980), 83.

19. L'Engle, *An Acceptable Time*, 89.

20. Ibid., 174, 185.

21. Ibid., 89.

22. Madeleine L'Engle, *The Irrational Season* (New York: The Seabury Press, 1979), 169.

23. Ross and Robins, *Druid Prince*, 134.

24. L'Engle, *An Acceptable Time*, 235.

25. Ibid.

26. Conway, *Celtic Magic*, 82.

27. Ross and Robins, *Druid Prince*, 35.

28. James Bonwick, *Irish Druids and Old Irish Religions* (Salem, N.H.: Ayer Co., 1984), 205.

29. Anne Ross, *The Pagan Celts* (London: B.T. Butsford, Ltd., 1970), 154.

30. L'Engle, *An Acceptable Time*, 152.

31. Ibid., 134.

32. Ross and Robins, *Druid Prince*, 133.

33. Bonwick, *Irish Druids*, 183.

34. L'Engle, *An Acceptable Time*, 55.

35. Ross and Robins, *Druid Prince*. 144.

36. Christopher Bramford and William Parker Marsh, eds., *Celtic Christianity: Ecology and Holiness* (Great Barrington, Mass.: Lindisfarne Press, 1987), 64.

37. Bonwick, *Irish Druids*, 200.

38. Lewis Spence, *An Encyclopedia of Occultism* (Secaucus, N.J.: The Citadel Press, 1960), 97.

39. Bonwick, *Irish Druids*, 173.

40. Ibid., 183.

41. Ibid., 71.

42. Manly P. Hall, *An Encyclopedic Outline of Masonic, Hermatic, Qabbalist and Rosicrucion Symbolic Philosophy* (Los Angeles: The Philosophical Research Society, 1977), XXIII.

43. Moore, "The Gnosis Interview," 20.

44. Ibid., 20-21.

Chapter 4: The Cathedral of St. John the Divine

1. Madeleine L'Engle, *A Circle of Quiet* (New York: Farrar, Straus and Giroux, 1972), 35.

2. Ibid.

3. Ibid., 170.

4. Ibid., 195.

5. Madeleine L'Engle, *A Severed Wasp* (New York: Farrar, Straus and Giroux, 1982), 88.

6. Ibid.

7. Madeleine L'Engle, "An Evening with Madeleine L'Engle: Readings and Dialogue," lecture given at Bethany Lutheran Church in Englewood, Colo. on 14 October 1989.

8. Madeleine L'Engle, *Walking on Water: Reflections on Faith and Art* (Wheaton, Ill.: Harold Shaw Publishers, 1980), 179.

9. Ibid., 186.

10. Ibid., 194.

11. Ibid., 171.

12. Ibid., 183.

13. Normon Beucher, "Miracle on 112th Street," *New Age Journal,* 11 (September 1986): 34.

14. The Cathedral of St. John the Divine Newsletter, 15 May 1991.

15. Ibid.

16. "Is That the Holy Water?" *New Age Journal* (January/February, 1991): 15.

17. Ibid., 35.

18. Norman Beucher, "Miracle on 112th Street," *New Age Journal*, 2 (September/October, 1986): 37.

19. " Building the Earth at St. John the Divine: A Gothic Cathedral Shapes a New World View and a Wider Vision of Humanity," *Tarrytown* (November 1984): 3-5.

20. *Valley Daily News* (22 April 1986): 41.

21. John Godwin, *Occult America* (Garden City, N.Y.: Doubleday & Co., 1972).

22. "Vexing Christa," *Time* (7 May 1985).

23. Ibid.

24. "Building the Earth at St. John the Divine: A Gothic Cathedral Shapes a New World View and a Wider Vision of Humanity," *Tarrytown* (November 1984).

25. Dr. Norman Vincent Peale, "What Freemasonry Means to Me," *New Age Magazine,* XCIV (May 1986): 4.

26. Madeleine L'Engle, *The Irrational Season* (New York: The Seabury Press, 1979), 201.

27. Jean Grasso Fitzpatrick, *Something More* (New York: Viking Penquin, 1991), 184.

28. "Building the Earth at St. John the Divine: A Gothic Cathedral Shapes a New World View and a Wider Vision of Humanity," *Tarrytown* (November 1984).

29. "The Green Cathedral," *Sequoia* (October/November 1990): 5.

30. Ibid.

31. Ibid.

32. Ibid.

Chapter 5: St. John's is Not Divine

1. "World Citizens Seek funds for 'Spiritual U.N.,'" *Shreveport Journal* (31 March 1962).

2. Ibid.

3. Ibid.

4. Ibid.

5. Letter from Daniel L. Anderson to an inquirer dated 22 August 1989.

6. William M. Bowen, Jr., *Globalism: America's Demise* (Lafayette, La.: Huntington House, 1984), 146.

7. Robert Muller, "A Cosmological Vision for the Future," *Goodwill Occasional Paper* (October 1989).

8. Michael McManus "Ethics & Religion" *Courier Gazette* (April 26, 1984).

9. "Voices of the New Age," Documentary on Public Television, (June 1992).

10. The Temple of Understanding Brochure (1982).

11. Ibid.

12. The Temple of Understanding Newsletter (Fall 1988).

13. Susan Gilmore, "National Interfaith Network is Set Up," *Seattle Times* (4 July 1990).

14. "The North American Interfaith Network," *World Faiths Insight Magazine,* 27 (February 1991): 28.

15. Ben Finney, "Ommm, Ommm, Ommm-ing with Gorby," *Mother Earth News,* 122 (March/April 1990): 60.

16. Ibid.

17.The North American Interfaith Network, *World Faiths Insight Magazine,* 28.

18. Dan Lehmann, "New World Parliament of Religions is Planned for Chicago in 1993," *Christian News* (13 November 1989).

19. John Cotter, *A Study in Syncretism* (Ontario, Canada: Canadian Intelligence Publications, 1983), 25.

20. The Temple of Understanding Newsletter (Fall 1991).

21. Ibid.

22. Ibid.

23. Ernest L. Boyer, "America Has Orphaned Its Young," *L.A. Times* (8 December 1991).

24. The Temple of Understanding Newsletter (Fall 1988).

25. The Lindisfarne Association Brochure (1992).

26. Ibid.

27. "The Lindisfarne Chapel," *Lindisfarne Letter* 12 (West Stockbridge, Mass.: Lindisfarne Press, 1981).

28. Ibid.

29. Paul Hawkin, *The Magic of Findhorn* (New York: Bantam Books, 1975), 215.

30. "The Lindisfarne Chapel," *Lindisfarne Letter* , 12 (West Stockbridge, Mass.: Lindisfarne Press, 1981): 10.

31. Ibid.

32. Dick Foster, "Beliefs Converge in Peace at Ranch," *Rocky Mountain News* (25 October 1987): 20.

33. Ibid.

34. Ibid.

35. "A Heavenly Garden," *Omni* 14 (March 1992): 34.

36. Madeleine L'Engle, *Two-Part Invention: The Story of a Marriage* (New York: Farrar, Straus and Giroux, 1988), 168.

37. L'Engle, *And It Was Good,* 82.

38. "Earth is Alive, Physicist Insists," *Rocky Mountain News* (13 November 1988): 22.

39. "Chilly Spring Belies Global Warming," *The Denver Post,* (7 June 1992): 17a.

40. Lawrence E. Joseph, "Gaia the Earth Goddess," *The Harmonist,* 2 (1987).

41. Ibid.

42. Ibid.

43. L'Engle, *The Irrational Season* (New York: The Seabury Press, 1979), 201.

44. Joseph, "Gaia the Earth Goddess."

45. *The Seattle Times* (11 May 1992): 8A.

46. "Time Will Test Impact of Summit," *Rocky Mountain News* (14 June 1992).

47. "Shaping a New World Order," *World Goodwill Newsletter* (3 November 1991).

48. *World Federalist* brochure (Summer 1991): 4.

49. David Segal, "Environmental Leopard Changes Spots," *Rocky Mountain News* (25 June 1992): 4.

50. Ken Armstrong, "Crestone: Pair Brings Together Dream and Its Means," *Valley Courier* (15 April 1987) 12.

51. "Rio's Legacy," *Time* (22 June 1992): 44.

Chapter 6: Contemplative Prayer

1. Madeleine L'Engle, *And It Was Good: Relfections on Beginnings* (Wheaton, Ill.: Harold Shaw Publishers, 1983), 135-136.

2. Ibid.

3. Albert James Dager, "Special Report on Renovare: Taking Leave of One's Senses," *Media Spotlight* (March 1992).

4. Dager, "Special Report on Renovare."

5. KLLT Radio interview between Richard Foster and John Loefler, on "Steel on Steel" (June 1992).

6. Richard Foster, *Celebration of Discipline* (San Francisco, Calif.: Harper & Row, 1978), 27.

7. Richard Foster, *Meditative Prayer*, (Downers Grove, Ill.: Intervarsity Press, 1983), 18.

8. Madeleine L'Engle, *Walking on Water: Reflections on Faith and Art* (Wheaton, Ill.: Harold Shaw Publishers, 1980), 86.

9. Foster, *Meditative Prayer*, 13.

10. Ibid., 27-28.

11. Ibid., 13, 15.

12. Ibid., 16-17.

13. Ibid., 9.

14. Ibid., 28.

15. L'Engle, *And It Was Good*, 136.

16. Ram Dass, *Journey of Awakening* (New York: Bantam New Age Books, 1978), 55-56.

17. William Johnston, *The Mirror Mind: Spirituality and Transformation* (San Francisco: Harper & Row, 1981).

18. *Valley Daily News* (15 December 1989).

19. *The New Encyclopedia Britannica* (Chicago: Helen Hemingway Benton Publishers, 1978), s.v."quietism."

20. Ibid.

21. Ibid.

22. Dave Hunt, *CIB Bulletin* ,7 (December 1991).

23. Dager, "Special Report on Renovare," 2.

24. Hunt, *CIB Bulletin* (December 1991), 2.

25. Dager, "Special Report on Renovare," 13.

Chapter 7: The Chrysostom Society

1. Philip Yancey, ed., *Reality and the Vision* (Dallas: Word Publishing, 1990).

2. Ibid.

3. Ibid.

4. *The New Encyclopedia Britannica* (Chicago: Helen Hemingway Benton Publishers, 1978), s.v. "John Chrysostom."

5. Herbert J. Thurton and Donald Atwater, *Butler's Lives of the Saints* (Westminster, Md.: Christian Classics, 1981).

6. Philip Yancey, ed., *Reality and the Vision* (Dallas: Word Publishing, 1991), 113.

7. Glenn E. Estes, ed., *The Dictionary of Literary Biography, American Writers for Children Since 1960: Fiction* (Detroit: Gale Research Co., 1986), s.v. "George MacDonald."

8. Yancy, ed., *Reality and the Vision,* 117.

9. Ibid., 152.

10. Joseph Campbell with Bill Moyers, *The Power of Myth* (New York: Anchor Books, Doubleday, 1988), 107, 222, 39, 68.

11. Yancey, ed., *Reality and the Vision,* 157.

12. Ibid.

13. Ibid., 155.

14. Ibid., 81.

Chapter 8: Comrades and Affiliations

1. "Playboy Interview: M. Scott Peck," *Playboy* (March 1991): 44.

2. "Peck's Path to Inner Peace," *Newsweek* (18 November 1985): 79.

3. M. Scott Peck, *The Road Less Traveled* (New York: Simon & Schuster, 1978), 283.

4. Ibid., 286.

5. Ibid.

6. "Playboy Interview: M. Scott Peck," 62.

7. Ibid., 56.

8. Ibid.

9. Ibid., 44.

10. "Peck's Path to Inner Peace," 79.

11. Tom Auer, "M. Scott Peck: Psychiatrist, Community Builder, Religious Thinker . . . Mystery Writer?", *Bloomsday Review* (January/February 1991): 11.

12. Ibid., 19.

13. Ibid.

14. M. Scott Peck, "A New American Revolution," *New Age Journal* (May/June 1987): 32.

15. M. Scott Peck, *The Different Drum: Community Making and Peace* (New York: Simon & Schuster, 1987), 215-216.

16. Peck, "A New American Revolution," 51.

17. "Playboy Interview: M. Scott Peck," 46.

18. Peck, "A New American Revolution," 51.

19. Joesph Campbell with Bill Moyers, "The Power of Myth" (New York: Achnor Books, Doubleday, 1988).

20. Ibid., 26-27, 40.

21. Ibid., 40, 107.

22. Ibid., 112.

23. Ibid., 45-47.

24. Ibid., 40.

25. Ibid., 86-87.

26. Ibid., 41.

27. Philip Yancey, ed., *Reality and the Vision* (Dallas: Word Publishing, 1991), 152.

28. Rosemary Guiley, *Harper's Encyclopedia of Mystical and Paranormal Experience* (San Francisco: Harper and Row, 1991), 605-606.

29. Dedria Bryfonski and Phillis Carmel Mendelson, eds., *Twentieth-Century Literary Criticism*, 9 (Detroit: Gale Research Co., 1978), 485.

30. Ibid., 484.

31. Ibid., 385.

32. Howard Hill, *How Did It all Begin?*, (Plainfield, N.J.: Logos, 1976), 32.

33. Madeleine L'Engle, *Walking on Water: Reflections on Faith and Art* (Wheaton, Ill.: Harold Shaw Publishers, 1980), 39.

34. Madeleine L'Engle, *A Stone for a Pillow* (Wheaton, Ill.: Harold Shaw Publishers, 1986), 75.

35. Marilyn Ferguson, *The Aquarian Conspiracy* (Los Angeles: T.P. Tarcher, 1980), 19.

36. Ibid., 50.

37. Ibid., 57.

38. Frank Morriss, "Conjuring Up Some Strange Spirits," *The Wanderer* (23 April 1985): 4.

39. Promotional brochure from ICCS.

40. Miriam Starhawk, *The Spiral Dance: A Rebirth of the Ancient Religion of the Great Goddess* (New York: Harper & Row, 1979).

41. Samantha Smith, "Magic, Sex and Politics: The Witch's Brew," *The Eagle Forum Newspaper* (August/September 1986).

42. Ibid.

43. William Rodarmor, "Original Blessing," *Yoga Journal* (November/December, 1986).

44. Charles Simpkinson, "In the Spirit of the Early Saints," *Common Boundary* (January/February 1992): 19.

45. Morton Kelsey, *The Christian and the Supernatural*. (Minneapolis, Minn.: Augsburg Publishing House, 1976), 21.

46. Ibid., 77.

47. Ibid., 57-58.

48. Ibid., 76-77.

49. Ibid., 75.

50. Ibid., 76-77.

51. Ibid., 72-73.

52. Morton Kelsey, *The Other Side of Silence* (New York: Paulist Press, 1976), 121-122.

53. Charles H. Simpkinson, "In Spirit of the Early Christians," *Common Boundary* (January/February, 1970): 22.

54. Kirkridge Retreat Center brochure (Spring/Summer 1992).

55. Fritjof Capra, *The Tao of Physics* (Boston: Shambhala Publications, Inc., 1975), 11.

56. Ibid., 12.

57. Ibid., 7.

58. Ibid., 12.

59. "Global Education Association Premises," *Breakthrough* ,10 (Summer/Fall 1989).

60. Ibid., 31.

61. Mike Hamer and Nathaniel Mead, "Finding Heaven on Earth," *New Age Journal* (April, 1990).

62. Ibid.

63. Johanna Michaelsen, *Like Lambs to the Slaughter* (Eugene, Oreg.: Harvest House Publishers, 1989), 37.

64. Antonio Moreno, *Jung, Gods, and Modern Man* (London: University of Notre Dame Press, 1970), 95.

65. Ibid., 80, 89.

66. Kirkridge Retreat Center brochure (1991).

67. Ibid.

68. Moreno, *Jung, Gods and Modern Man*, 84.

69. Ibid.

70. Raymond Bernard Blakney, *Meister Eckhart* (New York: Harber and Row, 1941), XV.

71. *The New Encyclopedia Britannica* (Chicago: Helen Hemingway Benton Publisher, 1978), s.v. "Meister Eckhart."

72. Peter Hebblethwaite, "Eckhart no heretic after all?," *National Catholic Reporter* (15 August 1986).

73. J. Gordon Melton, *New Age Almanac* (Detroit, Mich.: Visible Ink Press, 1991), 32.

74. Ibid, 10.

Chapter 9: The "Mythical Bible"

1. Madeleine L'Engle, *And it Was Good: Reflections on Beginnings* (Seabury Press, 1979), 202.

2. Madeleine L'Engle, *Many Waters* (New York: Farrar, Straus and Giroux, 1986), 168-169.

3. Ibid., 279.

4. Madeleine L'Engle, *A Stone for a Pillow* (Wheaton Ill.: Harold Shaw Publishers, 1986), 81.

5. Joseph Campbell and Bill Moyers, *The Power of Myth* (New York: Anchor Books, Doubleday, 1988).

6. Madeleine L'Engle, "The Mythical Bible," television program, "The Chicago Sunday Evening Club" (October 1991).

7. L'Engle, *And It Was Good*, 86.

8. L'Engle, *Walking on Water*, 73.

9. L'Engle, *And It Was Good*, 166.

10. Campbell and Moyers, *The Power of Myth*, 13.

11. Madeleine L'Engle, *The Irrational Season* (New York: Farrar Straus and Giroux, 1979), 159.

12. Madeleine L'Engle, *Sold Into Egypt: Joseph's Journey into Human Being* (Wheaton, Ill.: Harold Shaw Publishers, 1989), 57-58.

13. L'Engle, *The Irrational Season*, 137.

14. L'Engle, *A Stone for a Pillow*, 12.

15. Madeleine L'Engle, *A House Like a Lotus*, (New York: Farrar, Straus and Giroux, 1984), 76.

16. L'Engle, *Sold Into Egypt*, 215-216.

17. Ibid., 181-182.

18. Ibid., 232-235.

19. L'Engle, *The Irrational Season*, 112-114.

20. Madeleine L'Engle, *Camilla* (New York: T.Y. Crowell, 1965), 249-250.

21. Campbell & Moyer, *The Power of Myth*, 26.

22. Ibid., 40.

Chapter 10: Another Gospel

1. Madeleine L'Engle, *Sold Into Egypt: Joseph's Journey Into Human Being* (Wheaton Ill.: Harold Shaw Publishers, 1989), 20.

2. Madeleine L'Engle, in speech given at Calvin College (23 September 1987).

3. Madeleine L'Engle, *The Irrational Season* (New York: Farrar, Straus and Giroux, 1979), 212.

4. Ibid.,112.

5. L'Engle, "Star-Gazer" (video) (New York: Ishtar Films, 1989).

6. L'Engle, *The Irrational Season*, 83.

7. Madeleine L'Engle, *A House Like a Lotus* (New York: Farrar, Straus and Giroux, 1972), 260-261.

8. Madeleine L'Engle, *A Stone for a Pillow* (Wheaton Ill.: Harold Shaw Publishers, 1986), 23.

9. Madeleine L'Engle, *And It Was Good: Relfections on Beginnings* (Wheaton Ill.: Harold Shaw Publishers, 1983), 30.

10. L'Engle, *Walking on Water*, 180.

11. L'Engle, *A Stone for a Pillow*, 12.

12. Shirley MacLaine, *Out On a Limb* (New York: Bantam Books), 107.

13. Helen Schucman, *A Course In Miracles* (Tiburon, Calif.: Foundation for Inner Peace, 1985), 32.

14. L'Engle, *A Stone for a Pillow*, 22-23.

15. Ibid., 209.

16. Ibid., 22.

17. L'Engle, *The Irrational Season*, 88.

18. L'Engle, *And It Was Good*, 162.

19. L'Engle, *A Stone for a Pillow*, 117.

20. Schucman, *A Course in Miracles*, 30.

21. Helen Schucman, *A Course in Miracles: Manual for Teachers* (Tiburon, Calif.: Foundation for Inner Peace), 47.

22. Madeleine L'Engle, *Trailing Clouds of Glory: Spiritual Values in Children's Books* (Philadelphia: Westminster Press, 1985), 23.

23. L'Engle, *The Irrational Season*, 3.

24. Ibid.

25. Ibid., 184.

26. Schucman, *A Course In Miracles*, 439.

27. L'Engle, *The Irrational Season*, 173.

28. Ibid., 164.

29. L'Engle, *A Stone for a Pillow*, 166.

30. Ibid.

31. L'Engle, *The Irrational Season*, 184.

32. Ibid.

33. Ibid., 60.

34. Ibid.

35. Ibid.

36. Ibid.

37. Elizabeth Clair and Mark L. Prophet, *Lost Teachings of Jesus*, (Livingston, Mont.: Summit University Press, 1986), 23.

38. L'Engle, *Walking on Water*, 81.

39. L'Engle, *And It Was Good*, 19.

40. L'Engle, *Walking on Water*, 20.

41. L' Engle, *Stone for a Pillow*, 195.

42. L'Engle, *The Irrational Season*, 97.

43. Ibid., 215.

44. Madeleine L'Engle, *Camilla* (New York: Ty Crowell Co., 1965), 251-252.

Chapter 11: Another Christ

1. Joseph Campbell and Bill Moyers, *The Power of Myth* (New York: Anchor Books, Doubleday, 1988), 173.

2. Madeleine L'Engle, *Cry Like a Bell* (Wheaton, Ill.: Harold Shaw Publishers), 47.

3. Madeleine L'Engle, *Walking on Water: Reflections on Faith and Art* (Wheaton Ill.: Harold Shaw Publishers, 1980), 20.

4. Madeleine L'Engle, *Sphinx at Dawn* (New York: Seabury Press, 1982).

5. Tom Auer, "M. Scott Peck: Psychiatrist, Community Builder, Religious Thinker . . . Mystery Writer?" *The Bloomsbury Review* (January/February 1991).

6. Madeleine L'Engle, *Sold Into Egypt: Joesph's Journey Into Human Being* (Wheaton, Ill.: Harold Shaw Publishers, 1989), 20.

7. Madeleine L'Engle, *The Irrational Season*, (New York: Farrar, Straus and Giroux, 1970), 71.

8. Ibid., 169.

9. Madeleine L'Engle, *A Stone for a Pillow* (Wheaton, Ill.: Harold Shaw Publishers, 1986), 201.

10. Madeleine L'Engle, *And It Was Good: Reflections on Beginnings* (Wheaton, Ill.: Harold Shaw Publishers, 1983), 58.

11. L'Engle, *Sold Into Egypt*, 20.

12. Ibid.

13. L'Engle, *The Irrational Season*, 135, 187.

14. L'Engle, *A Stone for a Pillow*, 86.

15. L'Engle, *And It Was Good*, 69.

16. L'Engle, *The Irrational Season*, 82.

17. Ibid., 167.

18. L'Engle, *And It Was Good*, 51.

19. Madeleine L'Engle, *A Wrinkle in Time* (New York: Farrar, straus and Cudahy, 1962), 89.

20. Madeleine L'Engle, *Trailing Clouds of Glory: Spiritual Values in Children's Books* (Philadelphia: Westminster Press, 1985), 106.

21. L'Engle, *A Stone for a Pillow*, 101.

22. L'Engle, *The Irrational Season*, 71.

23. L'Engle, *The Glorious Impossible* (New York: Simon & Schuster, 1990), 31.

24. Ibid., 37.

25. Madeleine L'Engle, *Two-part Invention: The Story of a Marriage* (New York: Farrar, Straus and Giroux, 1988), 193-194.

26. L'Engle, *A Stone for a Pillow*, 90-91.

To inquire about a newsletter updating information on the New Age Movement, write:

Samantha Smith
P.O. Box 322
Littleton, CO 80160

e. 103

ORDER THESE HUNTINGTON HOUSE BOOKS !

_____	America Betrayed—Marlin Maddoux	$6.99 _____
_____	Angel Vision (A Novel)—Jim Carroll with Jay Gaines	5.99 _____
_____	Battle Plan: Equipping the Church for the 90s—Chris Stanton	7.99 _____
_____	Blessings of Liberty—Charles C. Heath	8.99 _____
_____	Cover of Darkness (A Novel)—J. Carroll	7.99 _____
_____	Crystalline Connection (A Novel)—Bob Maddux	8.99 _____
_____	Deadly Deception: Freemasonry—Tom McKenney	7.99 _____
_____	The Delicate Balance—John Zajac	8.99 _____
_____	Dinosaurs and the Bible—Dave Unfred	12.99 _____
_____	*Don't Touch That Dial—Barbara Hattemer & Robert Showers	9.99/19.99 _____
_____	En Route to Global Occupation—Gary Kah	9.99 _____
_____	Exposing the AIDS Scandal—Dr. Paul Cameron	7.99 _____
_____	Face the Wind—Gloria Delaney	9.99 _____
_____	*False Security—Jerry Parks	9.99 _____
_____	From Rock to Rock—Eric Barger	8.99 _____
_____	Hidden Dangers of the Rainbow—Constance Cumbey	8.99 _____
_____	*Hitler and the New Age—Bob Rosio	9.99 _____
_____	The Image of the Ages—David Webber	7.99 _____
_____	Inside the New Age Nightmare—Randall Baer	8.99 _____
_____	*A Jewish Conservative Looks at Pagan America—Don Feder	9.99/19.99 _____
_____	*Journey Into Darkness—Stephen Arrington	9.99 _____
_____	Kinsey, Sex and Fraud—Dr. Judith A. Reisman & Edward Eichel (Hard cover)	19.99 _____
_____	Last Days Collection—Last Days Ministries	8.95 _____
_____	Legend of the Holy Lance (A Novel)—William T. Still	8.99/16.99 _____
_____	New World Order—William T. Still	8.99 _____
_____	*One Year to a College Degree—Lynette Long & Eileen Hershberger	9.99 _____
_____	*Political Correctness—David Thibodaux	9.99 _____
_____	Psychic Phenomena Unveiled—John Anderson	8.99 _____
_____	Seduction of the Innocent Revisited—John Fulce	8.99 _____
_____	"Soft Porn" Plays Hardball—Dr. Judith A. Reisman	8.99/16.99 _____
_____	*Subtle Serpent—Darylann Whitemarsh & Bill Reisman	9.99 _____
_____	Teens and Devil-Worship—Charles G.B. Evans	8.99 _____
_____	To Grow By Storybook Readers—Janet Friend	44.95 per set _____
_____	Touching the Face of God—Bob Russell (Paper/Hardcover)	8.99/18.99 _____
_____	Twisted Cross—Joseph Carr	9.99 _____
_____	*When the Wicked Seize a City—Chuck & Donna McIlhenny with Frank York	9.99 _____
_____	Who Will Rule the Future?—Paul McGuire	8.99 _____
_____	*You Hit Like a Girl—Elsa Houtz & William J. Ferkile	9.99 _____

New Title   Shipping and Handling _____
                                 Total _____

AVAILABLE AT BOOKSTORES EVERYWHERE or order direct from:
Huntington House Publishers • P.O. Box 53788 • Lafayette, LA 70505
Send check/money order. For faster service use VISA/MASTERCARD
call toll-free 1-800-749-4009.

Add: Freight and handling, $3.50 for the first book ordered, and $.50 for each additional book up to 5 books.

Enclosed is $_____ including postage.
VISA/MASTERCARD#_____ Exp. Date_____
Name_____ Phone: (____)_____
Address_____
City, State, Zip_____